MANUFACTURED
EDUCATION

MANUFACTURED EDUCATION

LEVERAGING COLLEGE TO ACCELERATE YOUR CAREER WITHOUT SELLING YOUR SOUL

Cimone Wright-Hamor, Ph.D.

Published by Best Seller Publishing®, St. Augustine, FL
Best Seller Publishing® is a registered trademark.
Printed in the United States of America.

ISBN: 978-1-962595-93-3

For more information, please write:
Best Seller Publishing®
53 Marine Street
St. Augustine, FL 32084
or call 1 (626) 765-9750
Visit us online at: www.BestSellerPublishing.org

Contents

Disclaimer

The information contained in this book is for informational purposes only. I am not an accountant or a lawyer or a health specialist. Any advice that I provide is my opinion, based on my own experiences. Any suggestions regarding dwelling or eating habits are strictly for cost-saving purposes, not for health or wellness. If you develop unhealthy eating practices which later affect your overall health, I will not be held liable.

The material within this book may include information, services, or products offered by third parties. Third-party materials comprise the products and opinions expressed by their owners, and I do not assume responsibility or liability for any third-party materials or opinions.

The third-party materials do not constitute my guarantee of any information, instruction, opinion, products, or services contained within the third-party material. The use of recommended third-party material does not guarantee success in your quest for a debt-free degree. The publication of this third-party material is simply a recommendation and an expression of my own opinion of that material.

Foreword

by Dr. Phabian, from the podcast
Listen to Me, I Have a Ph.D.

$433,841!

That is the debt I've accumulated over my 16-year journey in obtaining my Ph.D. The education system in the U.S. is no joke, and if you don't know what you're doing, or realize the options you have, you will face a situation

… (clapping hands to each syllable) … similar to mine.

Dear reader, I want you to remember this quote: "People with options act differently!" Ever since I left my first job out of school, I've lived by this credo. And guess who taught me this—no one but Dr. W, or as I refer to her, C-Monie!

I met Cimone during my final years of grad school as part of a community for black graduate engineers at Iowa State University. Our relationship developed in earnest the first few months after she and her family moved to the Tri-Cities in Washington, where we both worked at the Pacific Northwest National Laboratory. Conversations with Cimone usually went from zero to *Love and Hip Hop: Atlanta* intense, as she wanted nothing but the best for me and made sure I ALWAYS gave myself options when making any decision. It wasn't that I'd never done that before; it's just that now I am invariably aware of creating options in all aspects of my life.

Despite us both going through engineering programs—Cimone in computer engineering and me in both nuclear and mechanical—I couldn't help but notice how different our academic journeys were. A key difference was her debt-free experience and my "I can't buy a nice house in the early 2022 market" level of loan debt. Now, now … Don't let my situation deter you from pursuing a college education if that is your choice, because it is possible to do so debt-free when you know your options. How? Let me tell you more about my friend and how this college bible she wrote will help you.

A lot of people think they have time to figure things out in college, but the truth is, you don't. That's what I love about my discussions with Cimone. She doesn't dwell on problems; she jumps into solution mode. She'll say, "Okay, let's figure out how to get around that." This approach is the gist of this book. She sees issues associated with attending a university and jumps into helping YOU determine solutions by creating options for yourself.

When I say she helps solve problems, I don't mean a one-and-done situation. She'll text or call me out of the blue, and her sentence will begin with "I think if we do this …," and she'll start spitting bars like Snoop Dogg on *Wild 'N Out*.

I call her C-Monie because she understands money in a way that I still can't fathom. She spends time researching how the money flows in universities and realizes how similar their practices are to for-profit businesses. In tracking the money, she gets a better understanding of what needs to be done to provide you with some earnest cost-saving tips—things that I would not have thought about, and I was a financial aid peer counselor at a Big

Ten University … and I still graduated with a huge student loan debt (throws hands up in dismay).

In this book, Dr. W shares many stories about students not realizing their options and making costly decisions based on standardized information. As you are a first-time reader, I want you to spend time reading through the first three chapters. Reread, make notes, and review. This I found to be the foundation for your decision-making when contemplating college.

After reading this book you will gain certain fundamental knowledge. You will understand why college is nothing but a platform to further your goals. You will understand how to avoid the common business tactics used by colleges. You will understand traits that lead to debt when attending college. You will also realize there is a plethora of FREE resources that go to waste solely because someone isn't charging you for them. The book culminates with self-reflecting exercises and specific cost-saving tips not just for those thinking about going to college but also for those who are in the thick of it.

This book was meant for me 19 years ago. As a first-generation student whose family had migrated from Jamaica a few months before I started college, I did not know anything about U.S. finances, and I did not know much about the college process. All we had was the standardized rhetoric from financial aid counselors. Heck, I didn't have a computer until my first semester, so it wasn't as if I was able to search for information. Oh, and by the way, it was suggested I take out a student loan to buy that laptop, so I went with the suggestion.

YOU, my dear reader, are very fortunate, however, because not only do you have this information before you start this journey, but you have it in this easy-to-read book, and you have it for the rest of your academic journey. So, don't worry about me and my debt; Dr. W is already helping me with options to rid myself of it, because that's what she does, and I guarantee you she can do that for you too.

***Siri, play "Top Shotter" by DMX,
featuring Sean Paul and Mr. Vegas.***
—Dr. Phabian

Introduction

The BIG Ugly Event!

In a time of universal deceit, telling
the truth is a revolutionary act.
—George Orwell

Years ago, I began my journey toward a debt-free college degree. My journey led me to uncover the hidden truths about higher education that are often overlooked. This is NOT a book about college admissions. Instead, it's about optimizing your college investment, which requires intentionally designing a graduation plan and making informed financial decisions to minimize the cost of college. Take your time to understand the financial implications of your choices and adjust your plan as necessary. The information included in this book is practical advice, and I think you'll enjoy it.

Most people understand that we no longer live in an age where one can mindlessly wander through college without incurring debt. How should one navigate college? Colleges have a unique place in our society. When fully understood, they may help some people achieve their goals. Unfortunately, too many students go through college without understanding how they plan to leverage their college experience to obtain their desired outcome. Colleges and majors are randomly selected and usually do not align with the student's purpose. Thus, the cost of the experience may not provide a good return on investment. In plain English, you might not get your money's worth.

Myron Golden once said, "Sometimes people don't like the truth, even though they long for it. Some people want to know the answer as long as the answer fits into their current way of thinking. So they're longing for the truth, but when you tell it to them, they don't like it." People long to hear the truth, but when you tell them the truth, and the truth doesn't fit into their current way of thinking, they get angry. People get mad because the fact requires them to change, when they want a quick solution. When the result isn't quick, they remain angry. Because that result does not align with their current way of thinking and everyday habits, asking them to change means that their actions are wrong and will not get them the outcome they want. We as humans like to think that we're brilliant, so we will believe any lie that aligns with our current reality.

Most people are like sheep and only want to do what they see other people doing. They jump on the bandwagon of whatever is popular now and, as soon as that changes, they jump on the next bandwagon. That's how we got here with student loans. A few people received degrees and attributed their later success to college. Suddenly, everybody believes that a piece of paper will make them successful. If you believe this to be true, wearing Jordan shoes should make me a top basketball player. To my knowledge, I am not one of the world's leading basketball players.

Unfortunately, they failed to mention that those successful people were intentional about why they needed a college degree and selected their respective institutions. Only the ones committed to taking the time to learn are successful.

As a student about to attend college, you must understand that learning how to navigate the financial decisions of college will make or break your financial future. Suppose you want to be respected by your peers and become an indispensable employee actively sought after by companies. In that case, you must be strategic about the college you attend. Many students think the goal is to get to college, but that is far from the truth. The goal is to leverage college as a platform to accelerate your career. One way to measure success is to determine if the first job offer received because of your degree provides you with a livable wage. Here is the kicker: should you leverage college properly and start making an income before graduation, then you can decide if finishing the degree is worth it. However, most students need the degree to get a return on their investment.

Students must understand that this is a critical time in their life, so they must be strategic about selecting a major and targeting a profession. The lack of proper planning will most likely result in student loan debt. The odds will be in their favor if they choose to be strategic. They will satisfy degree requirements, graduate on time, and take ownership of their future. The student should always ask, "Is this helping me get closer to graduation?"

Families must pledge to be strategic and intentional about the college they select and recognize that certifications and multiple degrees may not yield the desired outcome. Therefore, choose the job you want and work backward to decide what major and certifications you may need to be qualified.

But note you are responsible for your success. If you fail to plan and make strategic decisions, you may drastically decrease the value of your investment. Acknowledge that accountability is a contract between you and yourself and carries no rewards or penalties for those who do not follow through. You need to be deliberate about your courses in the major you select to transform from a college student to an indispensable employee.

Many students get into college but never graduate. The number of students attending college versus those graduating is rarely shared. In a world where student loan debt has become the norm, planning out your college investment is essential. Long-term success never just happens by chance. It is always a result of clear objectives, focus, and diplomacy applied daily until graduation.

This book is for you if you want to get a college degree without breaking the bank and maximize your college investment. If your family is committed to your attending college without enormous debt, this is for you. This book is for you if you are enthusiastic and curious but unimpressed by generic college advice. Generic advice leads to large amounts of student loan debt, which most people pay until they are in their 50s.[1] Take time to learn how to navigate the financial decisions of college intentionally. If applied correctly, the principles in these pages will help transform your or your child's college experience and ensure you get the total value out of the investment. You will wonder how others accrued so much student loan debt by graduation.

During my journey, I learned valuable lessons that transformed my mindset about college and helped me obtain a bachelor's, master's, and doctoral degree without going into debt. Now I want to share my knowledge with others. I want to raise awareness about the severe threats of mindlessly wandering through college. Unfortunately, there is so much information compacted into this

---

[1]   Imed Bouchrika, "Average Time to Repay Student Loans: 2022 Statistics & Data," Research.com, October 5, 2022, https://research.com/education/average-time-to-repay-student-loans.

book that you will need to read it at least three times to help you avoid being exploited.

This book contains a wealth of information about adequately planning for college and will require highlighting sections you feel pertain to your situation. I recommend reading a maximum of one chapter per sitting to get the most out of the book. At the end of each chapter, there is a reference to a rap or R & B song that resonates with the chapter theme and helps you get into the right frame of mind. If you dislike rap or R & B, skip the song; it is not required to understand the book's material. To help you find your way, here is a quick look at how the book is organized.

The first part reveals how college is a business.

- Chapter 1 uncovers the essential business elements that directly impact the student.
- Chapter 2 defines college and confusing nomenclature.
- Chapter 3 details how marketing can cause people to consent without understanding the commitment of college.
- Chapter 4 discloses the hidden benefits of college and famous people who have leveraged the benefits to their advantage.

The second part of the book teaches how to optimize your financial investment purposefully.

- Chapter 5 explores the importance of having a purpose for the degree.
- Chapter 6 describes how to unveil your purpose.
- Chapter 7 walks through how to plan for college optimally.
- Chapter 8 breaks down how to fund a degree without going into debt.

This book may anger or disturb you if you do not want a more accurate perception of college. However, it will also drastically change how you see college; once you see it, it can't be unseen. Are you ready?

To your success,

Dr. W

**Siri, play "Successful" by Drake,
featuring Trey Songz.**

If you'd like to see if you're ready to navigate the college process, please visit ManufacturedEducation.com/checklist for complimentary checklists!

Chapter 1

DISCOVERING THE BUSINESS

Premature certainty is the enemy of the truth.
—Nipsey Hussle

STUDENT LOANS

In my junior year of high school, I witnessed the long-term cascading effects of student loan debt. I remember coming home from cross-country practice, and my mother's eyes were filled with tears. Like any concerned child, I wanted to comfort her and understand what was happening. So I wrapped my arms around her, and she explained that 25 percent of her paycheck was being garnished because she'd defaulted on student loans.

Moment of honesty: I did not understand most of what she said because I had no mental model of student loans or what it meant to default or garnish a percentage of someone's pay. But I would quickly feel the financial impact.

After finishing high school in '94, my mother attempted to get an associate degree from a community college. Unfortunately, she could not afford to pay for her education. While she had some scholarships, the remainder of her education was funded by student loans. Her schoolwork was going well; she excelled in all her math courses and her instructors were impressed. College was time-intensive, and child care was critical for her with two children under ten. However, she did not have the proper support and decided it was best to drop out of school and get another job to take care of her children.

She was forced to get two minimum-wage jobs to support her kids. She struggled to find a job that paid more. As a result, she could not afford to pay the student loan payment and cover basic needs. Therefore, she chose to forgo the student loan payments.

(In my SpongeBob narrator voice) "Ten years later …"

Now a single mom of three, with two high-school-age children and a toddler, she was barely making ends meet before the garnish. After 25 percent of her paycheck was garnished, we struggled to survive.

But wait, there's more!

We learned in the next tax season that the student loan service also seized tax refunds. She had been planning to catch up on some bills with that tax money. There were moments when the water, gas, and electricity were shut off all at once. Applying for government assistance was not an option. Government assistance did not consider the garnishing when deciding if we qualified for assistance.

Analyzing the Cost

The original student loan amount was about $3,500, but in the end, it totaled almost $40,000. My mom never finished her degree, nor did she do any work related to the degree.

Cimone's Message

When my family's only source of income was drastically reduced, we experienced some financial hardships. At times, these hardships seemed unbearable. Witnessing my mother struggling to provide because of defaulting on her student loan payments was eye-opening.

I realized at that moment that student loans severely set back finances. Student loans can drastically change somebody's life for the better or the worse; in our situation, it was for the worse. Arguably, this situation caused me some PTSD. I pay utility bills when they come available because I remember what it was like not to have lights and water.

College is a business, and student loans are one form of financial support for the business.

THEN CAME MY TURN TO ATTEND COLLEGE

Before applying to college, I knew my family could not cosign any loans or financially support me. My mom had defaulted on her student loans, and as a result, she was ineligible to cosign for anything should I need it. But my mother was not the only family member in this situation. I fully understood the situation and committed to obtaining all my degrees without going into debt. I was an enthusiastic beginner with little knowledge about how to proceed, but I was confident I could figure it out.

Off to college I went.

University Bookstores

I signed up to take the required chemistry course in my first semester of college. I assumed that $800 would cover the cost of all my books that semester.

It's worth noting that $800 was the random number I created without any cost basis. But every teenager thinks they know it all. You couldn't have convinced me that books cost over that amount even if you'd tried.

Monday, after class, I went to the campus bookstore and quickly learned that the textbook for my chemistry class cost $500. Without a doubt, I was ill-equipped to handle the sticker shock. I instantly began to vent in the store about how overpriced the books were, as if complaining would somehow lower the cost.

Shocked at the price, I searched for the author's name. To my surprise, I recognized it. My chemistry teacher was the author of the book. Unfortunately, there were no used copies available for sale.

I was forced to buy a new book to pass the class. This was my first direct experience with the business of college.

Analyzing the Cost

Professors usually don't get paid enough to cover the effort they put into teaching a class. As a result, they will find other creative ways to supplement their income, such as writing a book for the course they teach. Writing a course book can double a professor's income if the class is a required one. Now, this is not the case for every professor. The larger the publisher, the lower the royalty check for the professor.

The key to making book income into a dependable source is to create a new edition of that book every three to six years. Each new version contains changes and reorganization to render the previous versions of the book obsolete. The content will be organized in a different order such that if the professor gives assignments from the book by page, chapter, or exercise number, you are now completing the wrong assignment if you're using an old edition. At many colleges, professors are given the freedom to select which textbooks to use to teach their courses.

Cimone's Message

The cost of my course books disrupted my budget, and I had to use my small savings to purchase the remaining books. I learned the importance of getting multiple cost estimates to create an accurate budget. Books and materials for the first semester in college cost $1,200. This cost did not include purchasing a laptop. I was studying computer engineering without a personal computer.

College is a business, and part of the business is books.

TUITION AND TRANSFER CREDITS

Brett was an overachiever in high school. He took every advanced placement (AP) course possible in high school to shorten his time to get a bachelor's degree once he was in college. He transferred so many AP credits to his university that when he entered he was classified as a junior, which meant he'd accumulated at least 90 credit hours. Although he was classified as a junior, it took him an additional four years to graduate college.

Yes, you read it right. He was classified as a junior and still needed an additional four years' worth of credits to graduate with a bachelor's degree.

Here is where transfer credits get interesting. Although he could transfer all his AP credits from high school and achieve junior status in the university system, it did not decrease the number of credits necessary to get his bachelor's degree.

Analyzing the Cost

The naked truth is that only one of the AP courses transferred counted toward his degree program. However, this triggered differential tuition, which cost him an extra $15,000 on top of his expected bill. Ouch! One mistake cost him thousands. Hearing this story taught me that college is a business, and even when they allow you to transfer courses, those courses might not count toward your degree program.

Cimone's Message

Bringing unnecessary credits could also trigger other fees earlier than usual, costing you more money—one mistake becomes a multi-thousand-dollar penalty. This mistake cannot be reversed. Before you jump to get classified as a junior, make sure the courses you've taken count toward your degree program. The clout of being formally recognized as a junior may seem lucrative when you are a freshman, but it comes with a hefty price tag.

College is a business, and part of the business is tuition and fees.

PARKING PASSES AND TICKETS

Kensy was a sophomore in college when her mother had a heart attack. Suddenly Kensy was required to care for her three-year-old brother while attending class full-time, doing Reserve Officers' Training Corps (ROTC), and maintaining a part-time job. Additionally, she was expected to be physically present at the hospital where her mother was recovering, which was two hours away.

Pressed for time, Kensy requested a parking pass for the lot behind her dorm. To her surprise, the parking division denied her a parking pass, stating they had distributed all their passes for that lot. However, Kensy noticed open parking spots every night. She did not feel safe walking across campus at 3 a.m. and made an executive decision to park in the lot anyway. The first few nights, she did not get any parking tickets.

Her mom was in the hospital for a few months, and Kensy continued parking in the lot without the proper pass. She racked up $1,500 in parking tickets by the end of the semester. She ignored the tickets because her vehicle had not been registered with the university parking division and she did not believe they could figure out who owned it. However, when she initiated the process to renew the vehicle registration, she was told there was a hold on the account. The university parking division had put a lien on the vehicle's title for unpaid tickets, and Kensy was required to pay before she could receive license plates.

Analyzing the Cost

The cost of a regular parking pass was $100. Although she could not purchase a pass from the parking division, Kensy could have purchased a transfer pass for $90 from someone no longer using the parking spot. As a result, she wasted $1,410.

Cimone's Message

Universities make a substantial amount of money from parking passes and parking at stadiums during games. Most universities make millions of dollars from parking tickets annually, which is reflected in their budgets. In addition, most college campuses have a bus system. Unless you plan to live off campus, you may want to avoid bringing a vehicle to campus. Should you later need to get a vehicle, inquire about the various options available for parking and the multiple ways to purchase those options.

College is a business, and part of the business is parking.

MEAL PLANS

When I started college, I chose my meal plan based on the generic nutrition advice shoved down our throats in the public education system. Namely, everyone needs three balanced meals a day. So, I chose the meal plan that provided three meals per day. In addition, the dining facilities were open three times per day: breakfast was from 7:00 a.m. to 10:00 a.m., lunch was from 10:30 a.m. to 2:00 p.m., and dinner was from 4:00 p.m. to 8:00 p.m.

My course schedule was completely packed, as I took the maximum number of credits a first-year student could take. Therefore, my schedule was crammed with required labs and lectures from 6:00 a.m. to 7:00 p.m., from Monday through Thursday.

Fast-forward to the end of my first semester: I had over 50 percent of my meal plan remaining, and I figured I would get reimbursed for the unused meals. So I happily opened a browser and went on the university website to calculate the amount I would be reimbursed. According to the website, each meal in my plan cost $10, and I had just over 270 meals left.

The end of the semester came and went, and there was no refund. So during the first week of the second semester, I stopped by the accounts-receivables office to inquire about my refund. To my surprise, meals did not roll over, and there were no reimbursements. Any unused meals just disappeared. And I thought David Copperfield was an impressive magician; the university made that money disappear so quickly that I didn't even see it.

Analyzing the Cost
The operating hours of the dining facilities conflicted with my class schedule. Therefore, my chosen meal plan did not necessarily represent my availability to eat at the facilities. I wasted $2,700 on unused meals because I'd been reckless when choosing a meal plan.

Cimone's Message

My schedule prevented me from eating lunch and dinner in the allotted times that the dining facilities were open. Even ignoring my schedule conflicts, there was no logical reason for me to select a meal plan that provided three meals per day. I eat like a bird: a few crumbs and I'm full. I am very small, and I have never consumed three meals per day. Be reasonable about your dietary needs and consumption rate. Do not romanticize the meal options. After eating the same food for two months, you will not be as enthusiastic about the meal options as you were initially.

College is a business, and part of the business is meal plans.

CAMPUS HOUSING

Michael happily accepted his college admission offer. Eager to attend college and get the whole experience, he decided to stay on campus his first year, in one of the most popular dormitories. Like most other first-year students, he arrived with his family, who helped him move in and settle. However, Michael would soon learn that his dormitory was overbooked and there were no alternative living spaces in town.

The university's grand solution was to convert the community areas on each floor into sleeping quarters. These community spaces were shared by four students and included two bunk beds and four closets. Michael was very cooperative with the residential assistant who managed his floor, as he only wanted to enjoy his freshman experience. However, Michael and the other students living in the community space were required to pay the same total amount as if they were in a two-person room.

This housing shortage taught me that college is a business, and housing is part of the business. If you live on campus and choose to live in what they call a traditional-size dormitory, you will be forced to have a meal plan. These business models go hand in hand.

Analyzing the Cost

Michael paid $8,327 for a two-person dormitory room and received a four-person temporary living space. According to his university, a quad-dormitory costs $5,100. He lost $3,227 by not contesting the rate he was charged for the accommodations.

Cimone's Message

Don't assume that the bill you receive is always correct. If you paid for something and did not receive it, make sure to get the price adjusted accordingly.

College is a business, and part of the business is housing.

ATHLETES ARE CHEAP LABOR

Tyson was a star wrestler and received a full-ride scholarship. His ability to obtain a college degree was contingent on his wrestling scholarship. At the end of his first wrestling season, he broke his leg. He was dropped from the wrestling team, the school pulled his scholarship, and he was hit with a tuition bill, all within 48 hours of being discharged from the hospital for his wrestling injury.

His medical expenses were covered, but the remainder of his education was not. He quickly learned that his tuition was double that of in-state students. He was confused, stressed, and in pain—and without a job, he had to scramble to figure out how to afford the tuition.

It was at this moment that he realized the impact of his situation. He had been working out six hours per day and keeping a strict diet, and he was expected to report his whereabouts to his coach multiple times throughout the day. Now he felt cheated and abandoned. He'd spent years mastering his craft and becoming one of the top athletes in the nation, only to have it all ripped away. Tyson was offered an opportunity to rejoin the team should he fully recover. However, the situation caused him to rethink his future. He decided against trying out again for the team and instead changed his major from business to software engineering to increase his chances of postgraduation employment.

Analyzing the Cost

Tyson's projected out-of-pocket costs for college were $0. His actual out-of-pocket expenses were $152,357. Tyson did not have this money and was forced to take $62,357 of student loans to cover the expense. Additionally, he worked a job to cover the remaining costs.

Cimone's Message

Tyson banked his entire college career on being able to wrestle. While college sports may seem exciting, many factors must be considered. Athletes get a lot of free clothes, but their time is locked up, and they cannot work a job. Furthermore, unless they are a D1 athlete playing basketball or football, they are most likely not getting a stipend, so they have no spending money. In other words, they are the world's entertainment but receive little to no pay, and the benefit or hope of becoming pro is very slim. While that has changed recently, it has only changed for select individuals playing a few sports.

Through Tyson's experience, I learned college is a business, and sports are one of the ways schools make money. They make money off the athletes' performance. They make money from the parking at these events and from sales of the athletic clothing. The athletes are not compensated for the number of people they can rally and bring to the games or for the tickets sold. The athletes do not get any kickbacks.

College is a business, and part of the business is athletics.

COLLEGE IS A BUSINESS

College is a business, and every business has a cash-flow statement. Unknown to many, colleges have a cash-flow statement too. In business, the people who pay the most are those who do not know how the business works. Therefore, you must strategize to survive and sustain yourself. Attempting random things usually will not result in a positive income. There are many moving levers in this business. These are the main items the typical student must pay for: books, college tuition and fees, parking, meal plans, housing, and athletics.

In the business of the college, there are two types of families or students: 1) those who think like a consumer, and 2) those who think like a business. The consumer mindset will have you believe that student loan debt is normal, and you'll be able to repay it later. These individuals are often mindlessly drifting through college and will accrue a significant amount of student loan debt. The business mindset, however, will help you understand that there must be a clear alignment between going to a university for its benefits and ensuring that it is a win-win situation for both the university and the student. The main difference between consumer and business mindsets is that a student with a business mindset intentionally navigates college with goals, whereas a consumer follows a standardized plan provided to them by the university. That average plan is given to every student; if blindly followed, the student will most likely graduate with an average amount of student loan debt. Without someone there to help them stand out against their peers, these students will also likely struggle to communicate the value they can add to a company after graduation. Thus, these students will ultimately struggle to get a job. Although you came to college to increase your chances of a better life, don't abdicate the responsibility of your career.

The next chapter will challenge some common assumptions about college and reshape how you view higher education. This will lay the foundation for changing what you know and highlight the dangers associated with attempting to make things *equal* for all.

Siri, play "A Lot" by 21 Savage, featuring J. Cole.

Chapter 2

THE MISEDUCATION OF THE MASSES

If you are not willing to learn, no one can help you. If you are determined to learn, no one can stop you.

—Unknown

Earning a college diploma is touted as an achievement that will guarantee a livable wage. However, unrealistic expectations and misconceptions lead to disappointments, which may cause people to reject what they do not understand. Let's explore some of these misconceptions.

COLLEGE MISCONCEPTIONS

1. The Degree Is the Goal

A degree is just a piece of paper. I will print you one on high-quality paper if you are set on having it. However, I highly doubt that it will get you employed. The general population tends to think of a degree as a way to represent the fact that one has acquired foundational knowledge in a particular field. This perception is inaccurate. Unfortunately, many colleges have systemized their courses such that memorizing facts may be sufficient to pass the course. As a result, one could obtain a degree without critical-thinking skills.

The goal is to use college as a platform to accelerate your career, which means you obtain a job offer before graduation. A job offer before graduation requires demonstrating skills and experience (e.g., in internships, co-ops) in a related role. Note that I did not state that one is required to work for someone else. Entrepreneurship is always a viable option, although some people want to work for an established company to have a more reliable income stream.

2. A Degree Will Guarantee You a Job

Many people believe a college degree will guarantee a job. That may have been the case decades ago, but in today's world it is not true. A college degree is essentially insurance against your career and provides the theory behind the field. But that theory is just miscellaneous knowledge. The student must learn how to organize that knowledge to achieve the desired outcome, and most people get lost at this step. This step requires creativity and critical thinking. One must dream big, start with the few resources available, and think critically about how to acquire anything else one may need.

The K–12 public education system does not permit students to flex their creative muscles. However, in college, students must exercise their creativity, organize information, and teach themselves new information. But many of them struggle and genuinely expect to be taught the knowledge and techniques they need to obtain their goal. We'll talk more about this in a later chapter.

3. I Need an Advanced Degree to Make Six Figures

It appears that the more educated someone is, the more money they make. However, here is a quick lesson in statistics: correlation does not imply causation. This means that although people with more degrees appear to make more money, they are not necessarily getting paid more simply because they have a degree.

Other factors also come into play, and other statistics are required to determine the factors in earning a high income. Jumping to conclusions is highly discouraged and may lead to poor investments as a student. Research the field you plan on going into before making a commitment that you believe will result in a six-figure salary. Students often expect unrealistic entry-level salaries or go into fields that will not be hiring in five years. When they struggle to find the opportunity they are seeking, the college is blamed.

Criticizing a college does not seem appropriate, because the student made a voluntary choice. Their decisions may have been uninformed, but I have yet to hear anyone say that a college representative forced them to pursue higher education. These are life lessons, and accountability is essential to personal development; the lack of it breeds entitlement.

For example, John purchased a Peloton bike for $2,700 plus the subscription training program. Peloton has a 30-day money-back guarantee that states if customers do not get results, the company will provide a full refund. The program requires that John work out four times a week, but he worked out only once a week every other month. At the end of the program, John was dissatisfied with the results, so he posted a bad review of the bike. The reality is, he used the bike to hang his clean clothes on for 30 days.

John failed to drop weight, but not because the bike did not work or because the program was unrealistic. He failed to exercise as directed by the training program. Most would agree that John's lack of results has nothing to do with the bike. So do not blame college for your lack of job security and career progress. The inability to complete goals demonstrates a lack of self-respect.

4. College Isn't a Requirement for Success

The tech industry has created unrealistic salary expectations because it has become known for providing entry-level employees with six-figure salaries. Additionally, the industry has become known for not requiring a college degree. There are multiple ways to enter the tech industry, such as by attending college, completing a boot camp, or obtaining certifications. However, these paths do not provide the same benefits. In short, college teaches theory; boot camps teach a tool; and certifications verify that you know the jargon and concepts for a specific discipline.

College provides more theory behind a chosen field, which becomes essential when trying to innovate. Boot camp is an initial indoctrination that teaches basic, step-by-step instructions for beginners. Some boot camps are centered on teaching the material necessary to pass certification exams, but this is not always the case. A certificate is a piece of paper to prove fundamental knowledge of a product or field. Unfortunately, some programs are dedicated to teaching strategies that help people pass the certification exams without a comprehensive understanding of the material, which defeats the purpose of the certification. As shown in the table below, an individual boot camp is typically more affordable than a four-year degree and takes less time to complete.

Multiple Ways to Get into a Technology Career			
	College	Boot Camp	Certification
Theory	x		
Skill	x	x	
Product		x	x
Technical Jargon Time to Complete	x	x	x
Cost	$120K+	$2K–$25K	$500–$1K
Time to complete	2–4 years	12 weeks	4 hours

None of these teach you how to organize information to achieve a goal. Instead, through experience (internships, apprenticeships, and jobs), you will begin to learn how to arrange facts to create a blueprint to execute. All these data sources have a purpose, but the benefits are not the same. More importantly, none of these options guarantee job placement. Achieving job placement is heavily dependent on support from the organization and the work the client invests. College has benefits that are marketed using language that the average high school student does not comprehend.

Let's formally define *college* before we get into the details. Below is a list of various definitions of *college*.

WHAT IS COLLEGE?

According to Merriam-Webster, *college* is:

1. A body of clergy living together and supported by a foundation. (This is interesting. Can we find a college not supported by a foundation? This is more evidence that it's a business.)

2. A building used for educational or religious purposes. (This is vague. Does a church count as a school? Now that I think about it, if you look up the taxation for a foundation and a church, it's so low I wouldn't mention it.)

3. An independent higher-learning institution offering a general studies course leading to a bachelor's degree.

Synonyms: brotherhood, congress, consortium, fellowship, fraternity, league, organization, society, or a guild.[2]

According to Dictionary.com, *college* is:

1. An institution of higher learning, especially one providing a general or liberal arts education rather than technical or professional training.

2. A constituent unit of a university, furnishing courses of instruction in the liberal arts and sciences, usually leading to a bachelor's degree.

3. An endowed, self-governing association of scholars incorporated within a university.

---

[2]   Jetta Carol Culpepper, "Merriam-Webster Online: The Language Center," *Electronic Resources Review*, 2000.

4. Related words: association, institute, organization, alma mater, halls of ivy.

Notice that these definitions involve a group of individuals coming together for a common purpose supported by financial means, such as a foundation or endowment. In plain English, colleges bring like-minded individuals together and are one of the most common forms of a mastermind group.

The financial support suggests that there is some formal structure, and there must be some cash flow. You have to pay to be a part of this exclusive group. But a college and a university are not the same thing.

IS A COLLEGE DIFFERENT FROM A UNIVERSITY?

Technically, yes. But most Americans use the terms interchangeably.

According to Merriam-Webster, a university is "an institution of higher learning providing facilities for teaching and research and authorized to grant academic degrees. One is made up of an undergraduate division which offers bachelor's degrees and a graduate division which comprises a graduate school and professional schools, each of which confers master's degrees and doctorates."[3]

According to Dictionary.com, a university is "an institution of learning of the highest level, having a college of liberal arts and a program of graduate studies together with several professional schools, as of theology, law, medicine, and engineering, and authorized to confer both undergraduate and graduate degrees."[4]

---

[3] Jetta Carol Culpepper, "Merriam-Webster Online: The Language Center," *Electronic Resources Review*, 2000.

[4] Education, Special, et al. "Dictionary.com." Lexico Publishing Group. Accessed May 7, 2022.

Note that, based on the definition from the Merriam-Webster online dictionary and Dictionary.com, a university must have an undergraduate and a graduate program. Thus, the university must award doctoral degrees, the highest level of education in teaching and research.

The research aspect is often overlooked but imperative when considering college. A university is most likely focused on innovative contributions, meaning the rankings online are based on the number and impact of its publications. The rankings are not based on teaching, graduation, or job-placement rates.

From a technical point of view, *college* and *university* are not synonymous. The *college* definition mentioned nothing about the highest level of education. For example, a community college typically offers certifications and associate degrees but not doctoral degrees. Therefore, it would not be appropriate for a community college, such as Des Moines Area Community College (DMACC), to change its name to Des Moines University. Using the word *university* implies the institution awards doctoral degrees. However, this also means a university can have multiple colleges.

Let's use Iowa State University (ISU) as an example to show you how these two terms are related.

ISU has eight colleges:

1. College of Agriculture and Life Sciences

2. College of Design

3. College of Engineering

4. College of Human Sciences

5. College of Liberal Arts and Sciences

6. College of Veterinary Medicine

7. Graduate College

8. Ivy College of Business

Each college has multiple academic departments. For example, the ISU College of Engineering has eight academic departments:

1. Aerospace Engineering

2. Agricultural and Biosystems Engineering

3. Chemical and Biological Engineering

4. Civil, Construction, and Environmental Engineering

5. Electrical and Computer Engineering

6. Industrial and Manufacturing Systems Engineering

7. Materials Science and Engineering

8. Mechanical Engineering

FIGURE 1: A simplified organizational structure of Iowa State University.

A university has divisions that support all colleges. There are multiple divisions at ISU, including but not restricted to Student Affairs, Research, Academic Affairs, and Business Finance. The Division of Academic Affairs contains all the colleges.

ISU is not the only university with this structure; this is the general organization of a typical university. Now let's look at how college is a business using the Target Corporation as an example.

MINDSET SHIFT (LET'S CHANGE HOW YOU SEE COLLEGE)

Consider the following: you're in Target and you see a new drink brand you want to try.

1. You select the flavor
2. You put the drink in your cart
3. You purchase the drink
4. You try it
5. If you dislike it, you don't purchase it again

Now assume that you are attending a university and you see a major that interests you.

1. You select a course from that major
2. You add the class to your schedule
3. You pay tuition before the class begins, before you even know if the professor will be good or if you're going to like the class
4. You take the course
5. If you don't like the class or the professor, you don't take courses with them again

Process for Purchasing		
Organization	Target (Store)	University (College)
You select	New drink	New course
Add to cart	Add drink to cart	Add a course to schedule
Purchase	Pay for drink	Pay for tuition
Try it	Try drink	Try class

At this point, you should start seeing similarities between purchasing a drink from Target and purchasing a class from a university. Therefore, if you can recognize Target as a business, you should be able to acknowledge higher education as a business.

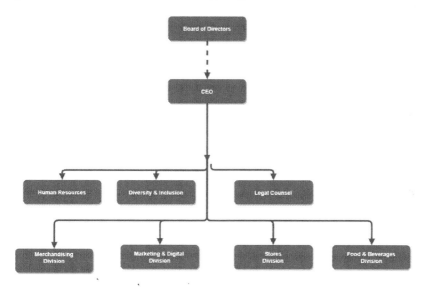

FIGURE 2: A simplified organizational structure of Target Corporation.

Look at Figure 2; notice that the corporate structure of Target has a position for diversity and inclusion, and a human resources department. Target also has a board of directors that governs what the CEO can and cannot do.

Take another look at Figure 1, the generic structure of a university. The structures of a university and a corporation are very similar. The university has a board, a president, a student affairs division, an academic affairs division, a business and finance division, economic development and industry relations, marketing, and so on. Also, notice that the university is governed by the board of regents or a board of directors, which controls what the president can and cannot do.

At this point, you should notice some similarities between Target's structure and the university's general structure. That is because, once again, a university is a business, not just a school. To be effective, the business/college has to track its finances on the balance sheet, and it must maintain cash flow to stay afloat. As described, there are two significant mindsets at play when people go to college: consumers and business owners.

Target has a CEO, and Iowa State University has a president. Both organizations have vice presidents, divisions, and departments. Using a different name, such as *university* or *college*, desensitizes people, but college has always been a business.

Similarities Between Organizations		
Organization	Target	Iowa State University
Roles	CEO	President
	VP	VP
Structure	Company	University
	Division	Division
		Colleges
	Departments	Departments

Colleges Are Brands!

Harvard is one of the most popular college brands in the United States. Ask anyone from the U.S. to name the top three colleges, and there is a high chance that they will name Harvard University. Harvard has over 300 trademarks. This is one of the most successful college brands, and their marketing has worked wonders. Just look at the number of students who want to attend solely because of the school's reputation. If that does not scream a business, then I do not know what does. By protecting their brand with trademarks, Harvard can prevent others from using their name without permission (i.e., without paying Harvard). Don't take my word for it; do a trademark search. There is a high chance that the college you are interested in attending is protected by a trademark.

When Did College Become a Business?

From an organizational standpoint, college has always been a business. When most public institutions began, they were funded by state and local governments, which may have helped control the price for students. This is not necessarily the case today;[5] state funding for many public institutions has drastically decreased.

In the 1960s, when the United States government decided to back student loans, it triggered something in the financial sector. Bankers use other people's money to make money, which is known as *leverage*. Additionally, banks do not like risk but do like guaranteed investments. As a result, for centuries, banks were not interested in student loans because there were no guarantees that students would repay the loans—until the United States

5   Sophia Laderman, *SHEF: FY 2017: State Higher Education Finance* (Boulder, CO: State Higher Education Executive Officers Association, 2018).

government stepped in and agreed to back student loans.[6] This reduced the risk to virtually nothing.

By backing loans, the government opened up the ability to fund higher education for families who did not have sufficient funds. Unfortunately, this shifted the financial burden from the institutions to the U.S. government. When the banks realized they could provide student loans without risk, they jumped on it. And the first few decades of banks provisioning student loans were brutal. College students from the 1980s and '90s amassed $200,000-plus in private student loans because interest rates were so high.

These students assumed they would make the unrealistic salaries needed to repay the loans. However, they did not understand how compound interest would impact their monthly payments. As a result, after making payments for ten years, many ended up owing more than they'd originally borrowed. To be clear, these students voluntarily accepted the terms but may not have understood the totality of the commitment.

CONSUMER VERSUS BUSINESS OWNER

If you are comfortable taking out student loans and then paying them back later, you are a consumer. A consumer purchases products and services and does not produce them. However, there are dangers associated with not taking time to accurately assess whether you need a product and the impact it will have on your life. Making such an assessment would empower you to control the price you're willing to pay.

---

[6]   Senate, U.S. "Sputnik spurs passage of the National Defense Education Act." *Senate Gov. https://www.senate.gov/artandhistory/history/minute/Sputnik_Spurs_Passage_ of_National_Defense_Education_Act.htm*

During adolescence, one of our deepest desires is to be accepted; colleges know this, and they build their marketing around the perception that we will be accepted. They send students emails and pamphlets, making them feel as if they are desired. Of course, most of that is automated, but they understand that the student has to feel they are wanted, regardless of whether the school will be a good fit.

Creative marketing has caused many people to think it's not marketing. As a result, people's guards come down, and they never critically assess the need for the product independent of what the salesperson has told them. Soon, they feel taken advantage of after discovering they have been told a half-truth, and the purchase is not exactly as they were led to believe.

Half-truths are a common way to market products. This occurs when information is purposefully omitted and facts are aligned in a specific order to prompt the consumer to assume things that are not true. The key is not explicitly stating these conclusions but organizing information to imply an "obvious" conclusion.

Many students who go to college and then graduate do not feel like they've been lied to. The truth is, the students were told that if they got a degree, they would be guaranteed a job with a livable wage that would allow them to pay back their loans with no problem. That is a half-truth. A college degree does not guarantee you a job, and you must use diligent planning to ensure that you have a job before graduation.

Furthermore, depending on your major and target job, you may not make enough to cover the student loans. Many students do not take the time to calculate the target salary for that particular job and the projected student loan payment. But it is essential for students to understand both numbers when calculating whether there will be a return on investment, not to mention understanding how student loans can cause financial ruin and why avoiding them is essential. A short section on the dangers associated with compound interest, which is the foundation of the financial market, appears later in the book. Compound interest impacts any financial loan, including student loans, credit cards, mortgages, and vehicle loans.

If you are not comfortable paying back student loans but want to ensure you get your value out of college, you must think like a business owner. A business owner will always tell you how a product impacts them in the long run and if they will get a return on their investment. When calculating your return on your investment, many factors must be considered.

To understand the factors influencing college investment, you must understand the market. When I talk about cost, I am talking about expenses to the students and their families; when I talk about price, I'm talking about the price listed by the university.

College websites provide price estimates, usually associated with their estimated cost of attendance. In this book, you'll find that the institution's cost of attendance is not an accurate representation of what the students and their families end up paying. As you understand, college is a business, and everything is negotiable. Most people are unable to pay the listed price. In this book, I will teach you more about thinking like a business owner and ensuring you have cash flow. Unknown to most people, careful planning can cut the college bill in half, and you can leave with a job offer before graduation.

VALUE IN COLLEGE

The average high school student does not understand the value of college and does not get their money's worth. College is a six-figure investment, equivalent to the price of buying a starter home in the United States. If you would not purchase a home without a real estate agent to guide you through the home-buying process, you should not send your child to college without an educational consultant to guide them. Four main benefits make college unique: 1) intellectual capital, 2) social capital, 3) financial capital, and 4) assets. These types of capital are often overlooked and underutilized. Paying someone to teach you how to use these benefits to your advantage is worth the investment.

The next chapter will cover how inaccurate information about college creates a false sense of job security. The false perception can result in a series of uninformed decisions and debt. This debt becomes a burden that is difficult to repay.

Siri, play "This Is America" by Childish Gambino.

Chapter 3

MANUFACTURED CONSENT

Emotions can certainly be misleading.
They can fool you into believing stuff
that is definitely, demonstrably untrue.

—Francis Spufford

Chole was a high school senior eager to begin her college journey. She applied to 15 schools, but one was more aggressive with its marketing than others. They sent her four times more mail and eight times more email than any other school. As a result, she felt they wanted her to attend their school more than did the other schools. Although the school didn't offer her as much financial aid, their constant advertising made Chole feel valued.

Chole attended this school and received a bachelor's degree in computer science. Unfortunately, her student loan debt for attending this private institution was just over $232,000 on graduation day. She would work for Microsoft with a starting salary of $88,000. The school had made her feel a false sense of financial security.

THEY TRACK YOUR DIGITAL FOOTPRINT

Many students attend college because they are told it is their golden ticket to a comfortable lifestyle. While this is not necessarily a lie, it is a half-truth. There are a few hidden assumptions that are rarely validated, and many of these assumptions are inaccurate representations of reality.

Marketing materials inspire many to believe they will have an unforgettable college experience or be entitled to a job.

Most people want a degree in order to obtain a job that will allow them to live their ideal lifestyle. In simple terms, people want financial security.

In full transparency, a degree does not guarantee job security; it acts more like insurance for your career.

Marketing can be very deceptive. Effective marketing is based on our deepest desires; thus, an ad will feel less like a sales pitch and will align more with the conversation in our heads. Social media platforms extract our deepest desires in a way that is not directly noticeable to the user. If you use Meta (Facebook and Instagram), Snapchat, or TikTok, you do not own the data you produce on these platforms. Therefore, the details you share about who you are, your interests, and videos or images can be used by the platform to create a marketing avatar. These platforms group similar avatars to create targeted marketing campaigns for businesses.

The pictures you post are often the most dangerous because facial recognition can be used to extract emotional responses to specific events. For example, selling a breakup song to someone going through a difficult breakup is easy.

College marketing campaigns are no different. They use many of these same mechanisms to market themselves and determine which students should be awarded more scholarships. For example, institutions that advertise on social media could use a digital pixel to track your information across multiple platforms. Your information is captured every time you interact with one of their digital assets (such as a website, Instagram ad, or email). Many institutions will hire external companies to create digital identification mechanisms for their digital assets. These companies record student data to gauge interest. Some go to the extreme of tracking your responses and communication with various parts of the university, including emails to the financial aid or the admissions office.

For example, if you go to a university website, there is a high chance the institution has a pixel embedded in the site that allows them to track your interactions with their site. This pixel captures information such as how often you visit the site, the pages you were on, if you read the entire page, and if you spent more time on certain sections than others. A summary of each student's activity is provided to the university and used to gauge interest in that school.

In the past, universities did not have the power leveraged from these trackers to understand or gauge a student's genuine interest. They were reduced to basic information submitted in the application form and the admission essay. If the institution does not have sufficient evidence that a student has a strong interest, they may not offer much financial aid.

Unfortunately, many students are unaware that colleges are tracking them. Therefore, students may not open emails from their top school because they are not accustomed to checking emails. As a result, that data is used against them.

I have witnessed many students wait until their campus visit to ask questions. They will demonstrate strong interest at that time, but that data is not captured. Without this data, you could hurt your chances of receiving enough financial aid to cover the cost of attendance. Periodically, students are verbally told inaccurate information that leads to a series of costly mistakes, and they have no proof of the discussion. Therefore, the discussion is hearsay.

It is one thing for someone to promise you something verbally, but it is another to have it in writing. People rarely get sued for saying something misleading. However, they are more often sued for writing down something misleading. Thus, all inquiries and responses must be in writing. You will find that people will recklessly state assumptions as facts verbally. However, when forced to write their response, there might be a discrepancy between what they said and what they wrote because most people understand that what they wrote could be used in court. Therefore, all requests should be in writing to serve as a source of truth.

WHAT IS THE WORST THAT COULD HAPPEN?

David completed his associate's degree at a community college because of generic advice from his high school academic advisor. The advisor told him it would be cheaper to get an A.A. and then transfer to a four-year university than to start at a four-year university.

He and his father went to the university to complete his paperwork and sign up for classes. At some point during the visit, they were separated. David thought nothing of it and continued to complete the tasks on his to-do list. He saved up the money to pay for his first year at the university but did not use it because he received another funding source to cover part of the first year. Instead, he worked during the subsequent summers to cover most of his tuition for the other years.

After receiving his A.A. degree, he assumed it would take an additional two years to get his bachelor's, but to his surprise, it took an additional three and a half years. By his calculations, he had incurred $20K in student loans. However, during his student loan exit counseling, he learned that his father had signed for a Parent PLUS loan on his behalf, for $16K, his first at the university. The Parent PLUS loan program was created by the U.S. Department of Education to lend eligible parents money to be used by their child for educational purposes. The loan was never disclosed to David until three years later.

David and his father met the financial aid officer separately. His father was told that David needed the loan for school, and without hesitation, his supportive father signed. However, when David met with the financial aid officer, he was told that his tuition and fees for the subsequent year were covered. While the financial officer's statement was not a lie, it cost David. He was unaware that loans covered his education and had saved enough money to pay for his first year of college. He was angry and frustrated because he had incurred more student loan debt than was necessary. The institution was later sued for deceptive financial aid tactics. However, David was not aware of the lawsuit and missed the deadline to participate in it.

Many families fall victim to similar situations, and this story is not uncommon.

MARKETING THAT DOES NOT FEEL LIKE MARKETING

Marketing today targets our deepest desires.

Companies create a comprehensive list of problems and the outcomes we want, then reshape their marketing materials to be the holy-grail solution to our problems, promising to deliver our desired outcomes.

This marketing works exceptionally well on teenagers because they have not mastered emotional control. Unfortunately, most teenagers are impulsive individuals. According to The Pollack Group, marketing to college students should have five elements: it should promote affordability, provide something for free, leverage social media, be humorous, and have a campus presence.

Colleges market the amenities more than the long-term bene-fits of a degree. Students tour the campus and become distracted by newly renovated workout facilities, a pool, and possibly even the gaming areas. Ironically, most students will never set foot in their campus gym after the campus visit. And people who don't swim will be excited to learn that the university has a pool. These amenities distract from the real value of college. People seem to forget that they have no intention of learning how to swim, as long as the pool and the workout facilities have the newest equipment in LED lights, surround-sound systems, and basketball courts that make you feel like you are in an Olympic arena.

Many students want to use the campus gym of my univer-sity, and I see people who spend more time taking pictures than doing any physical activity. I'm always reminded that it is more important to look like you are living a particular lifestyle instead of loving it.

Critical thinking becomes crucial at this point. College success means that you benefit more than the opportunity costs, which can be measured in many ways depending on the goal. But the return on your investment should always be positive. The most common reasons for going to college are[7]

- To improve employment opportunities
- To learn more about a favorite topic/area of interest
- To improve your self-confidence
- To learn more about the world
- To make a better life for your children
- To learn a skill[8]

Assume your purpose in going to college is to obtain a higher-paying job. Therefore, you must diligently track the cost of every semester and understand the potential income for your chosen career.

People buy with their emotions first and use logic to justify their purchase afterward. The top five motivators for buying are fear, love, greed, guilt, and pride, most of which are used in college marketing. For example, fear may insinuate that a college degree is necessary to live comfortably. While this may not be stated explicitly, the language used in the college marketing materials may imply that people without a degree do not live comfortably.

Income statistics about degrees held may be used to insinuate this claim further. According to the U.S. Census Bureau's Current Population Survey, *2020 Annual Social and Economic Supplement*, people with a high school degree made an average of $47,833, while those with a bachelor's degree earned an average of $84,896. The difference in pay may suggest that you are unlikely to make above

---

[7]   Rachel Fishman, *2015 College Decisions Survey: Part I, Deciding to Go to College*, Lumina Foundation, May 2015, https://www.luminafoundation.org/resource/deciding-to-go-to-college/

[8]   Hanneh Bareham, "7 Reasons to Go to College," Bankrate, August 21, 2022, https://www.bankrate.com/loans/student-loans/reasons-to-go-to-college.

$50,000 annually unless you have a college degree. In theory, the more education one receives, the more money one can make.

2020 Annual Social and Economic Supplement[9]	
Education Level	Average Annual Income, 2019 (US Dollars)
High School Diploma	$47,833
Associate Degree	$57,727
Bachelor's Degree	$84,896
Master's Degree	$106,841
Doctorate Degree	$158,549

THE AVERAGE SALARY STATS

Many colleges report the average salary for a new graduate. Therefore, you may see an advertisement stating "A student completing their bachelor's in computer engineering from our university makes, on average, a $150,000 salary." Salary statistics may lead students to believe that if they get a degree in computer engineering from this university, they will also make a $150,000 salary.

The truth is, some factors are not taken into consideration. These half-truths, a selected subset of facts strategically organized, lead one to assume a conclusion and align with a particular narrative.

The information presented in a half-truth is not false or wrong. However, half-truths prevent you from having a holistic view of the situation. Thus, they may create an inaccurate perception of reality.

---

[9] U.S. Census Bureau, Current Population Survey, *2020 Annual Social and Economic Supplement.*

The salary reported is not necessarily representative of reality because the number of computer-engineering graduates who respond to a salary survey may not strongly correlate with the number of graduates. In addition, the postgraduate survey is voluntary. Thus, the university's average may be a small subset of students. Furthermore, you must understand that the salary for that particular discipline may change drastically.

Unemployed or low-earning graduates may not respond. Some reasons a student may not respond to the postgraduate salary survey include embarrassment, shame, guilt, or anger. Conversely, some may lie or exaggerate their salary to make themselves feel more successful. Unfortunately, the salaries reported in these surveys are rarely validated, and colleges hope their graduates are honest enough not to inflate their salaries.

That is a significant assumption in the statistics presented by these departments. The statistics that departments may control, such as the average time for a student to complete their degree, have a higher chance of being accurate because these are data that they track and log independently of the student. But some statistics presented by universities use data that are rarely validated. The universities assume graduates have a high level of integrity and report truthfully.

ALL ABOUT THE BENJAMINS

Some people attend college to increase their earning potential. These students typically select a major based on whatever degree results in the highest salary. They train in that chosen discipline and use the university's network to ensure they get that highest-paying job.

These individuals are easy to spot because their résumés list a ridiculous number of clubs in which they are just members, thinking they'll be perceived as "doing more." They lack a commitment to their craft and talk only about money. These individuals exaggerate their contributions and perhaps are well spoken but less technical.

Inserting sarcasm: They are most likely to end up being your boss. Although I'm being sarcastic, there may be some truth to that statement.

UNPAID SWEAT JOBS

Some people go to college because they believe the more credentials, degrees, and awards they accumulate, the more recognition they will receive. These individuals are usually perfectionists who are head of their class and are featured in the college marketing materials.

Marketing materials are designed to make students feel like achieving a degree could bring their family many prizes and establish a legacy never known to them. Imagine getting a Ph.D. and becoming the first in your family to achieve it, with many patents and innovations impacting the world as we know it. Imagine the possibilities of going down in history and eventually getting a building on campus with your name on it. Unfortunately, most university marketing materials will hit one of these emotional buttons to be effective.

Often the marketing material is written to feel like a one-on-one conversation and to give the perception that needs will be met by getting a degree at their institution. Most students select an institution based on their emotions and justify their selection with logic after the fact.

Emotional decision-making can be an unsafe practice. As a result, most institutions analyze their target audience to understand which people are reacting to posts. Their ad will lead to the most significant benefit, which is usually emotionally charged. They use phrases that capture and hold the user's attention to help illustrate (in their mind) the possibility of having that benefit. These ads will be simple and to the point and will rarely discuss the details needed to help you achieve such benefits.

Students attend schools that do not align with their long-term interests or needs. Often they will select prestigious schools because of the clout behind them. For example, certain schools bring in rappers as a form of entertainment for their ideal demographic. Suppose a student wanted to be a rapper and decided to go to Iowa State University. Choosing to start a rap career at ISU would be a major mistake because the university's demographic does not typically value rap as much as other institutions do. ISU never brings in rappers to perform. As a result, selecting ISU would not be ideal for aspiring rappers hoping to start their careers by leveraging the college platform, and it indicates they did not correctly evaluate whether that particular college could help them start their rap career. If they were smart, aspiring rappers would do their research on the schools known for regularly hosting rappers to perform and for giving students the opportunity of performing as the opening act for a big-time artist.

Go back to the importance of understanding your purpose for this degree before choosing an institution. College is an environment where people with similar interests learn how to think, evaluate arguments, and synthesize information with respect to a particular field. However, one of the most common ways to measure if college is a lucrative investment is to track the job-placement rate and entry-level salaries. Obtaining a job unrelated to your degree may also be counted in job statistics. Note that is not the only value of college, but it is one of the common ways used to track the return on investment. There are other benefits of a college education, such as learning how to synthesize information, reason, evaluate arguments, and develop your mind. However, these are difficult to measure and track.

I am entertained by people who go to college and accumulate student loan debt to get degrees, only to end up in a job unrelated to their degrees. Unfortunately, it is common for people to get a job unrelated to their degree, which indicates the student had no purpose for attending college. These individuals often go to college because someone else told them it was a good idea, or they felt pressured into doing it because they did not know what to do next in life.

Inserting sarcasm: They probably mindlessly wandered through the degree program and did not have a focus or particular role in mind at any company they might work for in the future. Therefore, they chose some random degree program because it was interesting.

You should not choose a major if there is no defined need for its use. You must select an occupation and an organization to work for before choosing your major. By doing so, you constantly remind yourself of the end goal, which is never the degree. A degree is just a tool used to help you get to your purpose, which is the selected occupation at a particular institution. If you have not decided what your chosen profession will be and the specific institution you want to work for, you should not be selecting a major or a college, because neither guarantees getting you the job you eventually want.

You see this every day when people say, "I graduated with a bachelor's degree, and I do not work in that field." Often the same people accumulated a ridiculous amount of student loan debt because they had no purpose. They cannot articulate why they wanted a degree from a particular institution or how it would help them achieve their goal.

Nevertheless, students fall for the marketing gimmick.

When students visit the campus, it seems like a Disney experience. A fantastic tour guide shares random facts about the university and takes the students to all the campus attractions. But most of these facts do not help you reach your goal. For example, the guides may say, "This institution has been around for hundreds of years, and we have excellent graduates, such as this astronaut, that CEO, and even Elon Musk."

If it has not dawned on you yet, you must understand that the university's greatest asset is the product of its graduates. The university has clout only if its graduates give them something extraordinary. Now the college can create the perception that they contributed to the success of this individual. There may be some truth to that, but who knows?

The only thing necessary to note at this point is that universities and colleges will ride on the coattails of your accomplishments both during and after your attendance at their institution. This fact cannot be underestimated. You must understand that you are one of the university's most valuable assets because what you do after you attend this university, regardless of whether you get the degree or not, will often be used and incorporated into their marketing.

College marketing reminds me of new food blogs; at the beginning, the blogger shows a picture of a fully cooked meal and provides all the raw ingredients. Then they share their life story, which has nothing to do with the meal, and forget to provide step-by-step instructions and measurements, thus leaving it up to the new, inexperienced chef to figure out how to make the meal shown in the photo.

Karen, I don't care that your cat died when you were six. What does your cat have to do with making homemade biscuits?!

College can feel very similar to these cooking blogs. In the marketing materials, students are shown happy campus students participating in organizations, obtaining internships, and landing full-time jobs. However, there are no step-by-step instructions for how to be a successful student, obtain internships, and land full-time job offers. As a result, many students feel unsupported and unsure about the next steps, and they may drop out. The truth is, each student needs custom advice because each student may be at a different stage of development. Generalized advice without considering the students' background, life experiences, and context of their goals may lead to miscommunication or advice that is not actionable. Moreover, students will not understand the benefits of college or how to use them.

The next chapter will delve into the hidden benefits of college and how to get a return on investment. Most people think the ultimate achievement in college is getting a degree; this misconception may lead to issues. However, the real benefits are regularly televised using explicit language that the average high school student comprehends.

Siri, play "Cooler Than Me" by Mike Posner.

Chapter 4

LEVERAGING COLLEGE TO CREATE CHANGE

Make your intentions clear. The universe
does not respond well to uncertainty.

—Joe Duncan

There are many arguments against college, and most of the statements are half-truths. Half-truths are selectively chosen facts to cause someone to draw an inevitable conclusion without providing a comprehensive view of all the evidence. These data may be manipulated statistically to distort reality. It is a marketing technique often used by parents, friends, family members, and everyday people.

For this reason, you are highly encouraged to take a statistics course to understand how data can be manipulated. Without a comprehensive understanding of the data, you can create an inaccurate representation of reality, a half-truth. For example, you may have heard people justifying not attending college by referencing wealthy people who dropped out of college, such as Bill Gates, Steve Jobs, and J. Cole, and mentioning that LeBron James did not attend college.

These are true stories. However, they are half-truths. College can be a platform that provides intellectual, social, and financial capital and assets. If used properly, these benefits can help catapult your career.

BILL GATES (FAMOUS COLLEGE DROPOUT)

Bill Gates is a famous case used when justifying not going to college. I can hear it now: "Bill Gates dropped out of college, and he is one of the wealthiest men in the world!"

Gates is a founder of Microsoft, one of the largest tech corporations in the world. Chances are you have used a product created by Microsoft, such as Windows operating system, Edge web browser, or Bing search engine; a business communication platform such as Teams or Skype; a game console such as Xbox; or Microsoft Office products such as Word or PowerPoint. Now that you understand why Mr. Gates is a notable case, let us get back to the story.

Typically, when Mr. Gates is used in an argument against attending college, these critics fail to mention that Mr. Gates did not leave without using the university knowledge, resources, and network. During his year at Harvard University, he used the computer lab to build software that later became the first Microsoft product. The Microsoft founders used university resources as a complementary benefit of going to Harvard. Additionally, they used the university network to develop their business and leveraged the university's intellectual capital from its professors and networks to ensure that they could protect their business.[10]

In other words, Microsoft might not exist without Harvard University. The arguments people use about some of the wealthiest people in the world not having a degree are not wrong, but they are an inaccurate representation of reality. I am not arguing that you have to get a degree, but your chances of success without leveraging a college's benefits are minimal. Bill Gates and many wealthy founders did not finish college; they did not have a degree, but they leveraged the university's resources to create their wealth. And they're not the only people who have done this.

J. COLE (RAPPER)

If you want to be a rapper, your chances of success without leveraging college events are slim. J. Cole graduated from St. John's University with a bachelor's degree in communications and a minor in business. He had a 3.82 GPA.[11] He strategically selected St. John's because the college frequently hosts artists to perform as entertainment for the students. The Black Student Union (BSU) regularly schedules rap and R & B artists to perform there. The president of the BSU is responsible for planning the order in which artists perform at an event. When J. Cole became BSU president, he could schedule himself as the opening act for all the mainstream rappers. He strategically penciled himself in as the opening performer for the major artists. Additionally, the BSU president position comes with a scholarship.

---

[10] Walter Isaacson, "Bill Gates at Harvard," *Harvard Magazine*, November/December 2013, https://www.harvardmagazine.com/2013/11/bill-gates-at-harvard.

[11] "J. Cole First Interview/Freestyle After Signing to Jay Z and Roc Nation (Day After)," YouTube video, December 21, 2016, https://www.youtube.com/watch?v=rks3ub48O1k

There was a radio station on campus, and J. Cole was permitted to use the studio for free, which allowed him to produce his
music. He built his career using St. John's University as a platform.
In plain English, he strategically chose a university that could help
catapult his rap career to the mainstream. Today he owns a record
label and is one of the most prolific lyricists of our generation. J.
Cole is not the only rapper who leveraged college.

LIL WAYNE (RAPPER)

Most people are unaware that Lil Wayne had a 4.0 GPA in
psychology from the University of Houston (UH). Lil Wayne is
also known for using captivating metaphors in his music to express
his emotions so that his work instantly resonates with his fans. He
started his career performing at universities and clubs. In fact,
colleges host many events for student entertainment, and these
events are lucrative performing opportunities for young, upcoming
artists who likely have experiences similar to those of the students.
As the artists grow up and evolve, so do the members of their
fan base, thus creating and nurturing long-term relationships.
Although Lil Wayne did not complete his degree, he leveraged
college as a platform.

(In my Ron Popeil voice) "But wait … there's more!"

PROFESSIONAL BASKETBALL PLAYER

If you want to be a professional athlete, you will not get drafted
directly from high school. The competition pool is too big, so it's
tough to get noticed as an athlete by a professional team. At the
K–12 level, too many people dabble in sports and do it to occupy
their time. Some people are just not very serious about it, making
it difficult for a team to be successful if some of its members are

not dedicated to winning. When you get to college, though, the number of athletes drastically decreases. Although the competition pool is smaller than in high school, you are dealing with student-athletes who are dedicated to being an athlete.

Most NBA players were recruited from college. While some professional athletes don't complete their degrees before being drafted, they use the university platform to develop their skills and get noticed by professional organizations.

All NFL players are recruited from universities. As with basketball players, although some do not complete their degree before being drafted, they use the university platform to get noticed and perfect their craft. If you want to get drafted into the WNBA or into soccer, leverage the university to get seen. Many female athletes tend to complete their degrees before going pro. Long story short, most professional athletes leverage university resources to get noticed.

LeBron James and Kobe Bryant were among the very few athletes who were drafted directly from high school. Only 0.03 percent[12] of male basketball players in high school get drafted into the NBA. The chances of getting noticed increase drastically to 1.3 percent when players go to college.[13]

There are roughly 156,096[14] male seniors in the United States who play basketball; 0.03 percent of that number means approximately 46 high school seniors will get drafted directly into the NBA. In other words, a high school male basketball player would have to be number 1 in his respective state to get drafted directly from high school to the NBA.

---

[12] "How Many High School Athletes Get to Play NCAA Sports," College Sports Scholarships, March 11, 2016, https://www.collegesportsscholarships.com/percent-age-high-school-athletes-ncaa-college.htm

[13] Ibid.

[14] Ibid.

This is not the norm, nor should it be. Without the proper support, guidance, and development before starting a career as a pro athlete, people will be more likely to lose that opportunity because they are not ready for it. In 2005, the NBA created a rule to prevent high school students from being drafted, stating that the player must be one season removed from high school and at least 19 years old.[15] While no explicit rule states the player must attend college, it is to the player's advantage to go. If the player does not attend college, they risk falling off the NBA's radar. The NFL requires that players be at least three years removed from high school and use up their college eligibility to qualify for the draft, thus explicitly requiring players to attend college.[16]

MEDICAL DOCTORS (COLLEGE EDUCATION IS REQUIRED!)[17]

Being a medical doctor, lawyer, or engineer requires theoretical knowledge acquired at a deep level from a university. It is assumed that if you have a medical practice, a law practice, or an engineering firm, you have a certain level of accredited education. The knowledge and critical-thinking skills of these professionals have been tested and challenged. Otherwise, patients would risk being operated on by a doctor who does not understand how the human body works, which could cause issues, to say the least.

---

[15] "NBA Draft Rules," Lines.com, accessed September 29, 2022, https://www.lines.com/nba/drafts/rules.

[16] "The Rules of the Draft," NFL Football Operations, accessed September 29, 2022, https://operations.nfl.com/journey-to-the-nfl/the-nfl-draft/the-rules-of-the-draft.

[17] Office of Refugee Resettlement, "U.S. Medical Licensing Process," U.S. Department of Health & Human Services, June 18, 2012 (current as of June 11, 2019), https://www.acf.hhs.gov/orr/policy-guidance/u-s-medical-licensing-process.

SOCIAL CAPITAL (IT'S NOT WHAT YOU KNOW; IT'S WHO YOU KNOW!)

It does not matter if you want to be a rapper, singer, actress, professional athlete, medical doctor, lawyer, or engineer; you can use college as a platform to advance your career. There is no other organization with as extensive a network as a university. College networks have generations of graduates. Alumni can act as mentors or coaches and can open doors. There is a high probability that an alumnus can help you achieve your goals.

For this reason, once you decide what you want, you should reach out to your college's alumni association and ask for a list of people who have achieved that same goal. The alumni association's job is to track what former students are doing and keep in touch with them. In addition, alumni are loyal to their colleges and are more likely to give you an opportunity if they know you are associated with the same institution. They are more likely to offer you a job or share free information with you than they would with other people.

A level of camaraderie happens when there is a shared struggle in the same institution. Alumni assume that because you graduated from the same institution they did, you understand the battle and will have shared experiences; these act as an opportunity to build a relationship. Alumni have a bias toward fellow college graduates; but even though an alumnus has achieved your goal, it is unlikely that one person can provide you with everything you need.

Additionally, it is unlikely that an alumnus will be able to hand you a set of resources with everything you need, because that one person has not experienced everything possible. Therefore, it is advantageous to network with at least five people who have achieved your goal. They will all give you bits and pieces of information you need to move forward.

ACCESS TO RESOURCES

No other organization's members get offered as many free and discounted products as students attending college. Amazon Prime offers six months free for anybody who has a .edu email address.[18] Verizon gives discounts of up to 40 percent for students. Hulu and Spotify also give discounts to students.[19] Microsoft offers free Office products and Windows operating systems to all students.

If you have a .edu email address, your institution probably has Microsoft benefits. Learning to use the resources available to you could change your life. But finding a comprehensive list of all the free or discounted resources available is unlikely.

The list of free resources frequently changes. As a result, it is hard to create an up-to-date list. Do not assume. Always ask for any free or discounted resources available. To better understand the resources, you may need to do the following:

1. Decide on the target role and company, then use the university's social capital to determine the optimal career path and the skills necessary for the role.

2. Reverse engineer the role and identify resources needed to gain experience.

3. Ask university staff, faculty, and peers for free software available to students. The school may not have a special arrangement with a company to access software. In this case, go to that company's website directly and look for discounted or free opportunities for students.

---

[18] "Prime Student," Amazon.com, accessed June 21, 2023, https://www.amazon.com/amazonprime?ie=UTF8&hvadid=77859287117101&hvbmt=be&hvdev=c&hvqmt=e&primeCampaignId=studentWlpPrimeRedir&ref=pd_sl_6e5r-r9bsy_e&tag=mh0b-20

[19] "Student Discounts," Verizon.com, accessed September 29, 2022, https://www.verizon.com/featured/students.

Long story short, colleges have a lot of free and discounted resources, so check if a company offers discounts to students.

INTELLECTUAL CAPITAL

Intellectual capital, also known as collective knowledge, is another opportunity underused by students at college. This information is available from professors, instructors, administrators, and peers. Most courses require the instructor to have office hours, which often go unused by students. Students assume that office hours are restricted to learning class content, but this is far from true. Instead, consider using office hours for mentoring, and see them as an opportunity to connect with the instructor. Ask the professor about internships, full-time job opportunities, and scholarship recommendations to help you achieve your career goals.

It is beneficial to share your career goals and interests, as someone may be able to speak your name into existence in rooms and spaces where you are not allowed—trust that your network will help you get there. Additionally, professors' and administrators' knowledge could expose information not necessarily taught in class but often still needed to move forward. Insider information is intellectual capital on a deep level. Moreover, careers have unwritten rules never explicitly taught in a course. So please use professors' office hours and chat with administrators because these opportunities are free mentorship. Once a student graduates or leaves college, these benefits are no longer accessible or they cost thousands of dollars.

Furthermore, it has become prevalent for people to start online courses or platforms teaching this insider information. Often these platforms charge from $5,000 to $10,000 and sometimes even $50,000 to give you a small amount of information. However, this information is most likely available at a university, where the student will receive more knowledge, resources, and access to the network.

Select a college best suited to achieve your career goals, and apply for funding through scholarships, grants, and donations. Take note that universities with large endowments typically offer more funding to students. Degrees do not require you to incur debt. A degree is career insurance and proof that a student has obtained the minimum theoretical knowledge about a particular discipline. It is not a guarantee that the student will receive a job upon completion.

College is a platform with information, resources, and one of the largest networks in the world. A student can take advantage of these benefits without going into debt. Nevertheless, some students may decide that finishing a degree program will not be beneficial if they start making sufficient income before graduation. I do not think that college is for everyone. However, everyone can benefit from college in some form or fashion.

FINANCIAL CAPITAL (SOMEONE ELSE WILL PAY FOR YOU TO GET EDUCATED!)

Most students do not understand the benefits of college and how to use them, and most colleges and universities do not show students how to use these resources. In addition, many students do not realize that federal financial aid discontinues after roughly 160 credits. A typical bachelor's degree requires 120 credits.

From my experience, students who incur student loan debt start college without a clear purpose. These individuals change majors often; thus, they spend more time in college than their scholarships could cover. As a result, they rely on student loans. Student loans can jeopardize a student's financial freedom as an adult. Financial freedom is the ability to make decisions without cost influencing your choice. Additionally, these students often do not take internships, so they graduate with no real work experience, just a bunch of learned theories with no proof that they can apply them.

For example, Logan is a middle-aged man making $80,900 a year, and he has delayed having children because he has over $305,000 in student loans. Even with his spouse's income, they cannot afford day care and student loan payments. Often, these individuals did not apply for many scholarships or funding opportunities. In the past, college was cheap enough that people could work over the summer full-time and afford their tuition and room and board, but this is no longer the case. Back then, people would sign up for college, take a bunch of courses, and figure it out as they went because they could afford to pay that tuition bill without taking out loans. The cost of college was low enough. We no longer have that luxury. I would not recommend anyone go to college to figure out their life; it is too expensive.

The next chapter will examine the power of strategic planning and mentorship to increase your chance of success.

Siri, play "Level Up" by Ciara.

Chapter 5

INTENTIONAL AMBITION

When you control a man's thinking you do not
have to worry about his actions. You do not
have to tell him not to stand here or go yonder.
He will find his "proper place" and stay in it.
—Carter Godwin Woodson

If a college wanted to increase its graduation rates, it would reject anyone unable to communicate their purpose for obtaining a degree from that specific university.

This suggestion may sound harsh, but it may be more beneficial for students in the long run because they would be forced to create a vision for their future, including a clear need for the degree and institution. College today is so expensive that I would not recommend anyone attend it to find themselves. The process of self-discovery is never-ending, and the cost associated with not knowing what you want while taking classes is dangerous because self-discovery may cause you to change your career trajectory and significance. The key to getting a debt-free degree is choosing a career before selecting a school.

Unfortunately, too many students are indecisive. Their indecisiveness leads to switching majors and taking too long to complete their college degrees. Ultimately, indecisiveness leads to multi-thousand-dollar mistakes and ends in high amounts of student loan debt that is difficult to repay.

CAREERS AND LOYALTY (AM I STILL REQUIRED TO STAY WITH ONE COMPANY?)

Going after a college degree is a multi-year commitment, and you must not waver on that commitment. Once you decide you want to get a degree, do not change your mind. Understand that we no longer live in our grandparents' day, working full-time over the summer and earning minimum wage to cover tuition, or staying in a chosen career field until retirement. Millennials are expected to switch careers at least six times before age 65.[20] Choose a career, but understand you are not restricted to any particular career field; it is just a starting point. More importantly, you need to decide where you will start and build from there.

Once you pick a career, you need to reverse engineer the position. Select the position you want immediately following graduation, and find five job postings from at least three companies. Take the job postings and identify common skills or software that may be required for the role. Note the commonalities and interview people in the desired position to ensure that the commonalities you have identified are indeed the skill sets necessary for the job.

---

[20] "Apollo Technical: IT and Engineering Staffing and Recruiting Agency," Apollo Technical LLC, May 18, 2020, https://www.apollotechnical.com.

WARNING: Some job postings are a poorly written, inaccurate representation of the position, or they might have been copied from another company. Therefore, the skills pulled from the job descriptions must be verified by someone active in the field. Additionally, I have witnessed significant shifts in a chosen career field that are not yet transparent or commonly practiced. Therefore, it is vital to interview somebody who is already in that position and understands where the industry is going to ensure that the skill sets that you think are going to be necessary will indeed still be relevant by the time you graduate college.

The commonalities identified from job posts and interview data will be used to help you select the relevant skills. Additionally, take the time to select a particular position you want to pursue at a specific company. The target must be for a specific role at a specific company to be effective. All the information will be used to reverse engineer your career so you can get a full-time job offer before graduation.

THE BRAIN FILTERS UNIMPORTANT DETAILS

One must organize one's thoughts to have a clear and distinct purpose. Failing this can often lead to confusion and indecisiveness and to not completing the things you start. There must be a focus, and you should be able to succinctly articulate it. Identifying one's purpose is a process of continuous reflection and refinement. The average person does not reflect on the things that have happened to them long enough to identify a lesson learned. Thus, if you have not learned the lesson, you will continue to repeat the mistake until you have learned a lesson and the toxic behavior has stopped. Organize your thoughts, and you can control your attention.

When you control your attention, your brain acts as a filter. For example, when you get a new car, you start to notice that car more often. If you bought a gray 2008 Honda Civic coupe, it will feel as if suddenly everyone wants to be like you and they've also bought a gray 2008 Honda Civic coupe. You will start noticing the car everywhere, and you may genuinely feel like an influencer. However, statistically speaking, the same number of Honda Civic coupes were gray before you bought yours and afterward. Nevertheless, you have instructed your mind to filter for a gray 2008 Honda Civic coupe, and your brain will screen out any vehicle that does not fit those criteria. Hence, you start to notice that car more often.

Your chance of success works in the same way. Once you decide what role you want, the company you want to work for, the salary you want to make, and the date you want to start, your mind will find opportunities to make those criteria a reality. The subconsciousness will not submit to a weak level of conviction. If you are not committed to your goals, your mind will not filter or look for opportunities.

People who inject conditional statements into their goals demonstrate a weak consciousness. For example, they may say, "Our company would like to achieve a million dollars in sales this quarter if we could get $100,000 in marketing." But you never hear conditional statements like "If I can find my car, I am going to drive to the store." When people want to go to the store, they usually say, "I'm going to get in my car and go to the store." The idea is conveyed as a statement with no conditionals; the person is already committed in their mind to go to the store.

The same must be true once you decide on your target role and company. Of course, you can add more details to that goal, such as the salary, the ability to work from home, and perks like a MacBook or a Dell laptop. The more detailed you get about what you want, the better your mind can filter for that opportunity. But you have to decide and firmly commit to that goal. You must never waver. You might be unconvinced the first time you tell your mind about your plans. You will have to exercise your consciousness regularly to convince the subconscious of your level of commitment.

Most people think a degree is a goal, but it is not. If you believe the degree is the goal, I can print and ship you a college diploma on high-quality paper. In reality, the degree is just insurance for a career. If you have not chosen a career path, then you have effectively insured a nonexistent vehicle. For this reason, ensure that you have identified an ideal position at a specific company before starting college because this gives you a definite purpose. Then, when you know the motive and understand the role you want at a company, you can select a major that will best support you in that role.

You are essentially shooting in the dark if you don't have a target role and company. Mindlessly wandering through a degree program can cost you your financial freedom. Once you select a role at a company, take the time to learn that company's mission and values to ensure that they align with yours. Then, think through how you can articulate the alignment of your values with the company's values. Succinctly articulating the alignment of interests shows that you fit in with the organization's mission. Position yourself to become an indispensable employee.

The goal of college is to have gainful employment. Unfortunately, too many college students graduate without a job offer, which is dangerous. These students cannot articulate their desired role or the company they wish to work for. Subsequently, they are stuck with whatever is left over. This often leads to dissatisfaction with their job, depression, and a strong dislike for their employer.

Our most significant issues are no longer the external factors that block us from achieving our goals but rather the internal factors (such as beliefs, values, and self-talk) that cause barriers.

The beliefs you hold often limit your ability to execute tasks you are perfectly capable of doing. This is why it is dangerous to operate out of fear; it can result in extreme assumptions that are unlikely to happen. These extreme assumptions create a hostile environment that may not be real, but as long as the mind is convinced of the perception, it causes the body to operate in fight-or-flight mode. In this mode, the new information is not absorbed, and nothing is learned. The body is focused on fulfilling basic survival needs and experiences mental paralysis.

WHY MOST PEOPLE DON'T GET A RETURN ON THEIR COLLEGE INVESTMENT

There is an assumption that a person is entitled to a certain level of pay or employment because they have a degree. Full disclosure—a degree does not entitle them to either. College teaches the theory behind the field you have chosen to pursue. One precious lesson that I learned from physics was that although an object has the potential to do something, it may not accomplish it. However, the *possibility* of the object reaching its full potential is always there.

When I was a kid, I played with these things called frog poppers; they were plastic or rubber half spheres. Playing with the toy involved turning the popper inside out and placing it on a flat surface. Eventually, the popper would revert itself and spring up into the air.

I learned a precious lesson from playing with poppers. The surface affected how high the popper reached. Placing the popper on a plush carpet reduced how high it jumped. However, if I placed it on a hard, flat surface, such as a concrete floor, it would jump higher. And if I placed the popper on a flat finished-wood surface, such as a bowling lane, the popper would jump even higher than on concrete because there was less friction. The potential in the popper is the same despite the environment. However, the support needed to live up to its potential may not exist in that environment.

Much like a popper, each one of us has the potential to reach great heights. However, our environment may limit our opportunities and restrict our reach. Not every college is created equal. Therefore, when we choose one, we must be selective and ensure that it helps us achieve our goal. Failure to choose the right college that can adequately support us will result in our not reaching our full potential.

Knowing what we want to do is the first step toward selecting the right college and fulfilling our purpose. Determining the right college requires us to have a vision. According to Napoleon Hill, 98 percent of people cannot communicate their purpose. You are automatically ahead of most people by identifying a purpose for yourself and selecting a career that can help you achieve it.

WHAT'S PUSHING YOU TO CONTINUE?

A definite sense of purpose can be identified by understanding your motives. For example, in his book *Think and Grow Rich*,[21] Napoleon Hill notes that there are nine primary motives behind why we do the things we do:

1. Emotion of love
2. Emotion of sex
3. Desire for good health
4. Desire for self-preservation
5. Desire for freedom of body and mind

---

[21] Napoleon Hill and Mitch Horowitz, *Think and Grow Rich: Original Classic Edition. Reprint. (G&D Media, 2019).*

6. Desire for personal expression and fame

7. Desire for perpetuation of life

8. Desire for revenge

9. Emotion of fear

I find it interesting that these motives can often be linked to childhood trauma—they're driven by something we desired when we were children but did not receive.

There are five key ways to obtain knowledge:

1. Experience

2. Mastermind groups

3. Books or periodicals

4. Training courses or boot camps

5. College

Universities and colleges possess the most practical forms of general knowledge known to civilization. No other organization or institution has more general knowledge. Still, colleges have not perfected the ability to teach students how to organize that knowledge for a particular purpose other than for the assignments provided, which is why most students, out of frustration, say that their degree is useless. Students articulate that they learned a bunch of random facts but have no idea how to organize the knowledge to produce something valuable. This is where I come in—to guide the student.

THEY LIED! KNOWLEDGE ISN'T POWER!

Growing up, I was told that knowledge was power and was the key to opening doors. However, I later learned that knowledge was not power but only *potential* power. The power comes with organizing those random facts to produce value. In other words, we do not get paid for what we know; we get paid for the value we create from what we know.

Read that last sentence one more time to ensure you understand it.

Many people feel as if the educational system is broken, although I do not believe that is the case. You will find that these people typically have not identified their purpose, nor do they understand how to organize facts to achieve a desired outcome. They often expect free step-by-step guidance to achieve their goals but are unwilling to work for free themselves.

Intelligently organized knowledge creates practical plans of action to fulfill a specific purpose, requiring critical thinking. But unfortunately, too many people prefer to be told what to do than to consciously choose what to do.

The fact that a person has a college degree does not necessarily mean that person is educated. Students need to take the time to understand the random facts acquired in a classroom and organize them for a specific purpose, which should have been selected before choosing a major or an institution. Any student who cannot concisely articulate the purpose of their chosen major is at risk of failure.

A lack of purpose and of sound plans can promote feelings of inferiority, also known as imposter syndrome. If you suffer from this feeling of inferiority, your schooling has been limited, and your purpose is unclear. Remember, you are not restricted to the information you learn inside the classroom. Acquire facts from the other sources we listed above (such as from your own experiences and self-education, a mastermind alliance, a college or university, public libraries' supply of books and periodicals, and specialized training courses or boot camps).

No one source of information will give you everything you need. Students may assume that they will be able to acquire everything they need to be successful in their chosen discipline by going to college. That is a dangerous assumption that many people have. Assuming that a college can provide you with all the field knowledge you need to be successful in your discipline is unrealistic because that task is challenging, if not impossible, to do.

More specifically, it is impossible if you are in the tech field. The tech field changes procedures every six to nine months. Frankly, most of your professors have probably never been in private industry. Therefore, it is unrealistic to assume they can teach you everything you will need for your career. However, the information they teach you will give you enough theoretical understanding to advance in your chosen discipline and in ways that you may have been unable to access had you gone to a boot camp. Moment of honesty: if your focus is more on making money and belonging than on having a significant impact, college might not be valuable. It might be more impactful for you to attend a boot camp for a specific popular tool and get a six-figure job. On the other hand, if you long to make a lasting impact or you want to build a legacy in a chosen field, then going to college and learning the theory behind what you are doing may be more helpful.

Many boot camps do not include funding options, such as scholarships and grants. This means you will still have to pay the equivalent of a semester at university to get access to a fraction of the knowledge. That is the downside to boot camps that is not explicitly discussed. While there are free boot camps, getting into high-quality ones is challenging. The paid boot camps do not offer students the option of using government-backed student loans to cover the cost. Therefore, students are often stuck trying to scramble funding for a boot camp. All you can do is hope that the boot camp will be valuable enough to land you a job that provides the lifestyle you want.

WARNING: Some boot camps are led by inexperienced professionals, so do your homework before you pay thousands of dollars to attend.

Acquiring generalized knowledge from a college is like having a career as a doctor. The general practitioner knows a little information about a lot of different things. They do not make as much money as specialized doctors and, in many cases, are capped at around $300K.

A specialized doctor, such as a heart specialist, could make well over $500K. Why? It is evident when you should go to a heart specialist. You would never go to a heart specialist about a foot problem. The problem a heart specialist solves is obvious. What is the expertise of a general doctor? Nothing. A general doctor is the starting point for diagnosing many issues, and their job is to recommend a specialist. At the same time, general practitioners may have more patients than specialists. The specialist gets paid more because their time is efficiently used for patients with problems they have a higher chance of resolving.

Most companies want specialists, but not every specialization is treated equally. Many things are being automated, which is not necessarily bad. However, automation becomes difficult to accept when people have not done their due diligence to ensure their chosen field will still be viable five years from now. It makes them uncomfortable to think their job will no longer be something a human does.

As a result, whatever specialization you choose, do your due diligence to ensure the direction in which your occupation will be needed and, more importantly, understand the realistic salary for that chosen discipline. It would be unfortunate to learn that field has been significantly cut five years from now, and companies are not hiring, or worse, the occupation has been entirely automated. Improper planning for college can render the investment suboptimal.

Learning does not end at graduation. To truly master your craft, you must never stop acquiring specialized knowledge related to your primary purpose, business, or profession. The world is ever evolving, and we must evolve with it. At best, your college education will help you realize your optimal learning style and how to identify and acquire practical knowledge.

ANYTHING WORTH HAVING AIN'T FREE

I am amused by those who get angry about the cost of college. When I inquire if they took advanced placement or community-college classes in high school, they usually reply "no." Their response indicates that they had the opportunity to attend a public institution in education that was virtually free, and they did not take advantage of it. Now that they have to pay for the same education, most of which could have been free, they are frustrated and angry.

Anything acquired without effort and cost is generally unappreciated and often discredited. My self-discipline allowed me to capitalize on opportunities when knowledge was available without cost. The average person does not see value in something accessible. As a result, most people will not finish their degree or complete a free online course unless there is money and a deadline to create the urgency to finish promptly.

Take the online platforms Khan Academy and Udacity. These platforms have free courses, which are also offered at many universities and boot camps for a fee; but it has been found[22] that most people who start a free course never finish it. However, universities and boot camps have deadlines and hefty costs, and they also have a much higher completion rate than these free online courses with the same content. This validates even more that people do not value things until they put money behind them. For example, on YouTube, there are plenty of resources about starting a business and making money with little or no money to start. Moreover, I've seen tons of boot camps where people take the same material they found on these free YouTube channels and monetize them.

Most people start things and never finish them. Some people will go to college and change their major four to seven times. These people tend to graduate after ten-plus years and accumulate six figures of student loan debt only to accept a job unrelated to the degree. To make matters worse, they accept a job slightly above minimum wage, and now they are frustrated and angry because they cannot repay their student loan commitment.

This lack of planning is detrimental to your financial freedom. Throughout this book, you will hear me stress the importance of having a purpose and a plan. As you gain more experience, your purpose may evolve and reflect the lessons learned from these experiences. This is to be expected. As you grow as a person, it is extremely important to reflect upon your experiences, both good and bad, so you can refine your purpose and your plan.

The lessons you learn from your circumstances can be used to help someone else achieve their purpose and inspire them to do better. There is no fixed price for sound ideas. This is why colleges

---

22 Fiona Hollands and Aasiya Kazi, "Benefits and Costs of MOOC-Based Alternative Credentials: 2018–2019 Results from End-of-Program Surveys," *Center for Benefit-Cost Studies of Education*, Teachers College, Columbia University (2019).

can raise the cost of tuition to ungodly amounts, and people are still willing to pay it.

In the next chapter, you will learn how to find your values and explore your identity and interests to communicate your impact. At the core of every person is a set of values and priorities, known or unknown.

Siri, play "Imma Be" by the Black Eyed Peas.

Chapter 6

WHAT'S YOUR WHY?

A man without a purpose is as helpless
as a ship without a compass.
—Napoleon Hill

College students are inundated with an astronomical number of financial decisions that must be made within a few days. For many, the experience is almost unbearable, and students experience decision fatigue and make a series of costly mistakes. Without proper guidance to help them navigate the complexities of higher education, they risk incurring student loan debt, never graduating, and possibly never even pursuing a job in that field.

The exercises you go through in this book may require a lot of reflection and some time to process. Take the time, do your due diligence, be transparent and vulnerable with yourself, and be honest about your experiences and emotions. You can create a career that's not only fulfilling but also financially rewarding and impactful.

Unfortunately, most people never reach this point; they refuse to be vulnerable and honest about their past and experiences. Embrace your talents and the lessons that life has taught you. For every disadvantage, there is an equal advantage.

Too often, people wait to be chosen by someone other than themselves. For example, some high school students wait to define their worth based on the colleges that accept them. When admission letters start to roll in, they announce their acceptance to each college on social media. Many people will like, comment, and share the post in celebration, causing the student to feel accomplished. Everyone wants to be celebrated and recognized for major life milestones. However, I caution anyone who attaches their worth to acceptance to a college, as the selection process can be unfair and subjective. Your value is not based on which college offers you an admission letter.

Why wait? Why not choose yourself? Why does someone else have to choose you?

THE REAL COMMITMENT

College degrees are touted in U.S. society as a mark of achievement that gives instant respect. For example, when people meet for the first time, they often ask, "What do you do?" or "Where did you go to school?" Many people want a college degree, but few obtain one. The ability to complete goals increases confidence and demonstrates that honoring commitments to yourself is a priority. If you make commitments but do not follow through, it can decrease the trust level the subconscious mind has for the conscious. The subconscious will not trust any commitments made thereafter because, in the past, you have wavered on those commitments to yourself; what is to stop you from doing so again? A simple task such as getting out of bed immediately when the alarm sounds can be a major difference. These commitments are small but necessary to rebuild the trust between your subconscious and conscious mind.

Doing a task once or twice is insufficient. The subconscious must see a pattern to believe commitments are irrevocable. This means you must perform the actions consistently before feeling motivated. Contrary to popular belief, motivation does not come first. Suppose you mix this persistence with extreme emotion—your subconscious mind will receive your goal as a commitment you genuinely desire. In return, the subconscious mind will create plans for you to achieve that goal by identifying opportunities and only notifying your conscious mind of opportunities that will help you achieve your goal. It is not magic; it's energy, which cannot be created or destroyed.

This phenomenon is well understood by the most successful people in the world. There is an assumption that they've achieved their success by some luck or magical happenstance. But they have a clear purpose, are committed, and perform consistent actions that are measurable. Over time, you can track progress and see the improvements. Unfortunately, students do not seem to understand the power of tracking their degree progress and time to graduation.

TELL ME WHO YOU ARE, AND I'LL BELIEVE YOU!

At this point, you need to understand some things about yourself that must be true to have a purpose. Your identity is key to everything you are about to experience. Identities impact the lens through which the world is viewed. Chances are you probably haven't thought much about your character and values. However, now is the time to do so. This exercise aims to help you reflect on who you are and when you acquired each identity. This data will then be used to help clarify your purpose and long-term goals.

Complete the following categories:

1. Create an exhaustive list of identities, and try to be as specific as possible. Here are a few areas to get you started:
   a. Religious affiliations
   b. Age
   c. Gender
   d. Hometown
   e. Conditions (health conditions)
   f. Ethnicity
   g. Social and economic status
   h. Other identities

2. Create an exhaustive list of strengths. Most people do not know their strengths, as they're not well developed. Take the following quizzes to identify some characteristics or strengths you may have:
   a. CliftonStrengths[23]
   b. VIA Character Strengths[24]

3. What are your skills? See some of the examples below:
   a. Software development
   b. Writing
   c. Giving relationship advice
   d. Cooking
   e. Dancing

---

[23] "CliftonStrengths," Gallup.com, June 2, 2022, https://www.gallup.com/clifton-strengths/en/home.aspx
[24] "VIA Character Strengths Survey & Character Reports," VIA Institute on Character, https://www.viacharacter.org/.

4. What are your interests? Below are a few categories that may interest you.

   a. Basketball
   b. Comic books
   c. Science
   d. Gaming
   e. Social-media influencer content
   f. Health
   g. Art

5. What do people come to you for advice on?

6. What is your personality type? Take the following free quizzes to identify your personality type.

   a. 16Personalities[25]
   b. Myers-Briggs personality test[26]

7. List all your accomplishments and wins in life. Here are some categories to consider:

   a. Family-related successes
   b. Recognition and awards
   c. Degrees
   d. Sports

8. Now create a list of obstacles you overcame to achieve those accomplishments.

Your identity is the basis of who you are. Now, let's explore your identity. Although this exercise may seem like a lot of work,

---

[25] "Welcome!" 16Personalities, https://www.16personalities.com/profile.
[26] The Myers & Briggs Foundation, https://www.myersbriggs.org/.

this content will be used later as scholarship material. Complete the following:

- Select three of the subtopics (identities) shown above in the first list.
- Note your earliest memory about each of the three identities chosen from the first list.
- Write details about a situation in which you used a strength of yours, in reference to categories 2 through 5 above.
- Why do you believe this to be a strength? What is the impact of this strength?

Identities are more than physical attributes; they are also the values that you hold. Understanding your values will help you be consistent in how you behave. These quizzes will provide a short list of your strengths and identify your personality type. The key is to complete the quizzes quickly. The longer you think about an answer, the higher the chances of getting inaccurate results.

AM I ACCURATELY REPRESENTING MYSELF?

Validate the results of the quizzes with some of your friends or family to ensure the results accurately represent you. All categories above should start to display trends, which can help you identify a set of values. You will struggle and constantly feel lost without a clear set of values and identities. This feeling often leads you to being used by people who will leverage your lack of purpose and guidance for their benefit. Rarely will their influence benefit you.

By now, you should have a list of the following categories.

- Identities
- Strengths

- Skills
- Interests
- Personality type

Look for commonalities across the categories. Together, these things will be used to help you figure out your purpose. The idea is to list good and bad milestones to create a timeline. These significant events create a unique story around who you are. Find at least three friends and three family members to validate the results.

WARNING: This exercise can be nerve-racking, as you may hear things about yourself that are not ideal.

SHOULD I ALREADY KNOW MY MAJOR?

Some of the most annoying questions asked of students are
"What do you want your major to be?"
and
"What do you want to do in the world?"
These questions are loaded and usually result in unrealistic responses. This is equivalent to asking a five-year-old, "Who do you want to marry?" The child is most likely going to choose a popular celebrity. Realistically, what are the chances of a five-year-old being able to predict accurately who they will marry?

Similarly, asking teenagers what they want to do with the rest of their lives is just as unrealistic. For this reason, I strongly dislike these questions and find them unproductive.

A more appropriate question would be "**What problem in the world irritates you so much that you would dedicate your free time to resolving it?**" This question will lead to natural responses and reveal deep motivations. The answer to this question is a problem worth solving. Take time to honestly reflect on things that bother you and write down your responses.

Select one response to focus on—this will become your official problem to solve.

Now that a problem has been defined, let's go through an exercise.

1. Which companies are solving that problem? Leverage a search engine to find companies.
   a. Select one company from the list.
      i. Review the list of open positions for the company.
      ii. What position in that company do you think aligns with your interests and skill set?
      iii. Based on the job description, what major do you think would help you qualify for the role? The job description will usually specify which majors are ideal for the role.
   b. Using a search engine, look up universities with that major that are ranked in the top five.
   c. Select one college from the list. Go to the alumni association of that college and look for alumni who work at the selected company.
2. If you cannot find a company focused on solving your identified problem, consider starting an organization dedicated to resolving the issue. For example, if you cannot find a company that creates vegan dog food, you may be forced to start your own company.

I have provided a formal process for narrowing down critical decisions about college. Note that the process started with a problem and not a solution. The goal is to reverse engineer the role you want in the future. This will provide the reason behind pursuing a particular degree at a particular institution. When the coursework seems unbearable, quitting without a strong sense of purpose may seem like an appealing option. To prevent abandonment of your goal, you must establish a clear objective before you encounter difficulties.

LONE WOLF

The most difficult thing about getting a degree is that it gets lonely. You will find that certain people no longer add positive value as you evolve and will refuse to see that you have outgrown the version of yourself they once knew. The situation may even require you to distance yourself from certain people. This does not need to be a public announcement. There is no need to belittle people or discredit those who no longer exhibit the traits you wish to imitate.

There's a phrase that people say: "It's lonely at the top." When you become so focused on achieving a goal, you lose the ability to relate to people not pursuing similar goals. The lack of relatability may cause you to distance yourself. However, there will be natural gravitation toward those seeking similar goals. It will take some time to identify the people going along the same path—and you might not find any. Although your goals may be similar, your paths will not be identical. When two people share a similar focus and intensity, there will be a natural tendency to gravitate toward one another. However, if you fail to put yourself in environments where you can meet people with similar interests, you might have to pursue your goal alone.

There will be lots of time alone to reflect, progress, and achieve your goals. It will feel as if you have isolated yourself from the rest of the world. It may be challenging to interact with people to whom you cannot relate, as your mindset is fixated on something they have no experience with. The things you focus on and believe will change the energy you emit. The connection with old friends may weaken as your interests and priorities no longer align.

The further you achieve higher education, the less likely you'll be able to relate to those who do not strive for similar goals. The college experience forces extreme accountability and transformation that some will never fathom. As a result, you may struggle to connect with people with whom you once felt a bond. They will sense that you have changed and begin to distance themselves. As your interests and extracurricular activities change, old bonds will feel forced. When you transition to a job, the distance may increase with people you know who are not in a corporate position.

Whatever you choose to do, focus on it and pursue it relentlessly.

WARNING: Be careful about disclosing your plans to small-minded people.

IT'S A VIBE!

As you evolve, you will learn to become more sensitive to the vibes of others. Humans give off energy. When you come across someone who does not like you, you may be able to feel it. That vibe is not imaginary.

When someone does not like you, their magnetic field moves in the opposite direction of yours.[27] Therefore, your body will have to work harder to care for your basic needs when you are around them. When this occurs, energy will be taken from something to compensate for the extra energy to cover your basic needs. Remember, energy is not created or destroyed; it is transferred. Therefore, continuing to surround yourself with people who do not like you creates negative energy and can result in catastrophic

---

[27] Gerhard Baule and Richard McFee, "Detection of the Magnetic Field of the Heart," American Heart Journal 66, no. 1 (1963): 95–96, https://doi.org/10.1016/0002-8703(63)90075-9.

failure. Do your due diligence and ensure that the people you are around are uplifting you and promoting a positive experience.

Your closest friends and relatives can destroy your confidence through opinions and ridicule. We may live in the same building, but we don't necessarily have the same view. People can only imagine you achieving goals that they have achieved themselves. When people have a negative view of you, it is not about you. Their opinion is a reflection of their own insecurities. In plain English, they actively seek qualities they subconsciously believe they possess. When someone does not believe they can achieve something, they will find or search for that failure in other people. Do not get angry with these people, as they do not understand themselves enough to realize the power of the subconscious mind.

This often means you might have to work hard in silence and wait to disclose your achievements or forgo sharing them altogether. Prematurely disclosing your plans may cause some people to see you as a threat. You will need to acquire information discreetly without disclosing your purpose. Otherwise, some may take your plans and implement them out of envy.

HABITS: YOU ARE WHAT YOU DO

> *"Most of life is showing up. You do the best*
> *you can, which varies from day to day."*
> —*Regina Brett*

Your emotions do not accurately represent reality. Do not let them inhibit progress toward your goals. The mind is designed to resist anything that might seem harmful or difficult. Once the goal is set, you must achieve it.

Let me take a moment to explain the meaning behind the Woody Allen quote. The brain has a limited number of decisions it can make per day. Attempting to go over your daily limit will result in decision fatigue. For this reason, routines are key to reducing the number of decisions your brain is required to make. A routine is a sequence of events executed whenever a condition is met.

For example, you may have a routine of

1. Starting your day at 5 a.m.

2. Getting out of bed immediately the first time the alarm goes off

3. Putting on workout clothes

4. Grabbing a water bottle

5. Going to the gym

Perform these tasks consistently for 66 days. Your subconscious mind will recognize the pattern as something you have committed to doing and will automatically perform the sequence without requiring your conscious mind to make any decisions.[28] This means that no matter how you feel, you will get up, put on your gym clothes, go to the gym, and exercise because you have trained yourself to perform at a specific time every day. Therefore, 80 percent of success is just showing up to the gym. When you get there, you will automatically engage in physical activity and ignore any resistance you may feel.

The same process is valid for getting a college degree, starting a business, buying a house, or achieving any other goal. Once the mind has been programmed to do something, it automatically continues to execute the sequence whenever the trigger is initiated.

---

[28] Phillippa Lally et al., "How Are Habits Formed: Modelling Habit Formation in the Real World," *European Journal of Social Psychology* 40, no. 6 (2009): 998–1009, https://doi.org/10.1002/ejsp.674.

No matter how you feel, get up, dress up, show up, and never give up!

WHAT DO YOU WANT YOUR LEGACY TO BE?

When Bridget was in high school, her brother died from complications related to diabetes. The traumatic experience of losing her brother influenced Bridget to pursue biomedical engineering. After college, she worked for a start-up focused on creating affordable solutions to combat diabetes. Bridget's desire to prevent other people from suffering a diabetes-related death has pushed the boundaries of technology and impacted the world. Sometimes unfortunate life events and past experiences can influence our chosen career fields. Often these experiences serve as pathways for us and opportunities to help others who struggle with similar issues.

Circle back to our question: **What is something that bothers you so much that you would dedicate your free time to solving it?**

Ponder this question for a bit. Once you have selected a problem of reasonable size, choose a college major, based on your skills, that will help you solve the problem. Then, you can start to look for colleges that are best suited to position you to succeed. Remember, college is not free.

The next chapter will teach you how to calculate the total cost of a college investment and how the power of strategic planning impacts the final bill. The chapter will detail how to analyze the full cost of college and offer money-saving hacks. One of the core principles of financial planning is to understand how much money is needed to cover the bills.

**Siri, play "Bigger Than Me" by Big Sean,
featuring the Flint Chozen Choir and Starrah.**

Chapter 7

PLAN FOR SUCCESS INSTEAD OF GUESSING

If you've got a plan, it's not just like a
pipe dream. You have a step-by-step list
of things to do to get to your goal.
—Nipsey Hussle

At this point in working through this book, you have discovered a challenging problem to solve: identifying both an ideal company as well as a role within that company. Additionally, you should have selected a major that qualifies you for that role. I encourage you to create a list of institutions where that major is ranked in the top five. From this list, select one institution, and we will go through a detailed exercise to maximize the value of your college investment.

WESTSIDE STORY? IT WAS ALL A DREAM!

When I started college, I made friends with about 15 people. We created cohorts to help each other get our degrees; we thought everyone would graduate simultaneously and be lifelong friends. Little did I know that half the group would drop out by the end of the first year. The following year, another half would drop out. So, at the end of our college experiences, only four of us obtained our degrees.

What set me apart from my peers was that I had a detailed plan. Unfortunately, many students mindlessly stumbled through their degree program and followed the standard graduation plan. They did not have a custom plan to help them graduate. To be clear: they did not have an actual goal in mind. They genuinely believed all they needed to do was go to college and get a degree, and then a job would be waiting for them at the end. Many of them did not do internships during our college years. Their focus was more on getting good grades, joining clubs, and partying. They lacked a strategic plan.

They were living the dream, but unfortunately, that dream was short-lived. When I ask students today, "When is your graduation date?" the response is often an estimate. There is an issue here. I ask for a date, which includes a month, day, and year, but I receive a range. The inability to quickly answer the question often indicates little planning.

ALL MY CREDITS WILL TRANSFER!

Nicole was a transfer student who was told she could reduce the cost of obtaining her bachelor's degree by doing two years at a community college. She completed her last two years of high school taking dual-credit classes at a community college. She made her family proud by graduating with a high school diploma and an A.A. degree on the same weekend. However, Nicole would soon learn that the private institution she'd enrolled in did not accept dual-credit community-college courses.

Colleges set their own policies regarding transfer credits. Before taking any generalized advice, inquire about circumstances in which transfer credits are accepted and counted toward your degree program. A college may accept credits but not count them toward your degree program for graduation.

Why would they accept non-degree credits? This is a variation of the situation that happened in the "Tuition and Transfer Credits" section from Chapter 1. Accepting courses deemed as non-degree would increase the student's credit count. Seeing that a student's classification is determined by the number of credit hours earned, a student could be classified as a senior and still have four years until graduation. In fact, the student may invoke additional fees once they achieve junior status, thus resulting in the student unnecessarily paying more money.

Academic Advisor, Walk Me Through My Degree

Many students begin college believing that their academic advisor is responsible for ensuring they graduate—that the advisor's job is to facilitate the students' academic progression and help them satisfy graduation requirements.

But let's look at this from a more realistic standpoint. Most colleges have a four-year degree program, which is a plan that suggests the courses that should be taken for each semester over four years. The plan is generic and most likely was not created by the advisor using it.

Furthermore, the academic advisor most likely does not have a degree in the field they are advising you about. Additionally, they probably handle a high number of students. On average, an advisor has upward of 340 students.[29] Therefore, it's unlikely an advisor can give you unique, personalized advice.

Back in the day, academic advisors were the professors. However, when the student population drastically increased, there became a need to separate the professor role from the advisor role, and academic advising was outsourced. As a result, advisors no longer have degrees in the fields they give advice about, and any advice they offer the student is secondhand. It is a collection of information from professors, past advisors, and students who have already gone through the program. Therefore, the best place to get advice is from those who have gone through the same program.

Additionally, the academic advisor probably has hundreds of students to manage, given the number of students in a typical college and an advisor's standard 40-hour work week. It is unrealistic to expect that every student will receive red-carpet treatment. The chances are small that the advisor can focus on one student, complete a holistic assessment of their situation, and create a graduation plan that caters to their needs. Furthermore, the academic-advisor role is more comprehensive than just meeting with students. Please do not take my word for it. Look up some job descriptions for college academic advisors.

That said, most academic advisors I have come across are passionate about their job and try to help their students. However, they are limited in what they can do and how many people they can support. As a result, students' expectations around the academic advisor's role are overinflated and not backed with much support.

---

[29] "2011 Nacada National Survey," NACADA, https://nacada.ksu.edu/Resources/ Clearinghouse/View-Articles/2011-NACADA-National-Survey.aspx.

GRADUATION (START WITH THE END IN MIND)

Understand that your educational experience is your responsibility and a personal commitment. To be clear, an academic advisor is not responsible for ensuring you graduate. They cannot control the amount of effort a student puts toward their degree. In fact, on most college websites, there is a clause that states the academic advisor is not responsible for anyone's progression toward a final degree.

Likewise, it is not your family members', advisor's, or college's responsibility to guarantee you receive a job offer before graduation. Take ownership and seek help when needed. To get started, leverage the four-year academic plan provided by the department as a starting point. Then seek out others to critique the plan.

If possible, newer students should have upperclassmen review their plan. Upperclassmen can notice problems such as courses that shouldn't be taken together being grouped in the same semester. Furthermore, these students can provide essential advice about which professors to avoid and which to seek out. Their insider information may influence newer students about when to take classes and where to find additional resources. These upperclassmen will act as unofficial mentors. Each semester, find a new upperclassman to review your plan. Understand that the plan will evolve with time. The value of having an upperclassman give you feedback on your degree program is incalculable.

At this point, you have all the courses necessary to fulfill the minimum requirements to obtain a degree and the number of semesters it will take to meet graduation requirements. Now determine your graduation date. First, take some time to look up the previous six commencement dates to identify a pattern. Then use this pattern to predict your target graduation date and to calculate the days until then.

The profound thing I did to stand out in college was to articulate my graduation date and the remaining days until that date to every potential employer. Repeating the countdown of days provided a consistent reminder of priorities to my subconscious. As a result, I made progress every day, even if it was as small as one sentence for a homework assignment.

Remind yourself daily of the purpose of attending college. It is essential to slowly program the subconscious mind into finding a solution to every obstacle. Combining your goal with an emotional response increases the chances the goal is accepted by the subconscious mind as something truly desired. Once the intensity of your desire reaches a certain level, the subconscious mind will filter for opportunities and solve any problems.

HOUSING ISN'T FREE

Establishing a graduation plan and date may feel like a significant weight off your shoulders. However, some of the most costly mistakes have yet to be revealed. A considerable portion of the cost of college is housing. When you're selecting housing, it may be tempting to choose on-campus housing because it is convenient.

Austin, a freshman, chose the most expensive housing. For his first experience in living independently, he wanted luxurious amenities, most of which he did not use. He thus amassed $21K in student loan debt.

Austin chose to live in the most luxurious suite-style housing on campus for all five years he attended college out of state. The suite-style single room cost $10,185 yearly and required a meal plan. He purchased the most expensive campus meal plan, which cost $5,076. Annually, room and board cost $15,261. It took Austin five years to complete his degree, and his total room and board costs were $76,305.

Had Austin been more mindful of his needs, perhaps he would have decided he did not require suite-style housing. If instead he had selected a traditional dorm room and one roommate, his cost of housing would have been $4,725. His annual price for room and board would have been $9,801, totaling $49,005. Austin could have saved $27,300 if he had been more reasonable about his needs—and he would have avoided student loan debt.

So, take some careful time to understand your needs.

When Austin's brother, Cole, started college, their parents purchased a six-unit building for $300,000. They put down $10,500, and the monthly expenses for the building were $2,020.77. Cole lived in one unit; the other five units were rented out at $550/month, making the income for the building $2,750. Subtract expenses from income ($2,750−$2,020.77), and his parents had a monthly cash flow of $729.23.

By purchasing a multi-unit property, Cole's parents did not have to pay for rent. When Cole graduated, his parents sold the apartment building for $468,000. Without any additional support, Cole was able to obtain enough scholarships to cover the costs of tuition and school fees. Cole graduated in 2014 without any student loan debt.

Not All Dorms Are Created Equal — Ask Questions

Traditional dorm rooms feel more like shared apartment rooms. The rooms are equipped with a bed, a dresser, a closet, a chair, and a desk. Often, these dormitories have basement laundry facilities, which usually cost money. Laundry facilities are among the considerations that people overlook when choosing an independent living situation for the first time.

Here are some important questions:

- Will the room be shared?

- Are meal plans required?
- Are the laundry facilities free?
- Is there an additional fee for using the air conditioning?
- Is there a community bathroom? If so, how many people have access to it?
- Will the dormitory have 24-hour restricted access?
- Are guests permitted in the room overnight? Are they limited to a certain number of nights they can stay in the room?

Apartments Are Your Responsibility

Below are other factors that influence the cost of housing:

- Distance from campus
- Proximity to stores or clubs
- Available amenities (washer and dryer, dishwasher, pool, and so on)
- Number of rooms in the unit

The cost of housing usually increases as you get closer to campus. Therefore, living off campus can lower the cost of housing. However, there are other factors to consider before deciding on accommodation, such as transportation to campus and parking. Most universities have brokered a deal with public transportation allowing students to ride transit for free or at reduced fares. While public transportation may cost less than owning a vehicle, the additional commute time may not be favorable.

The amenities available in each housing situation will affect the cost. For example, a small apartment will often be cheaper if it does not have a washer and dryer. The opposite can be true for an apartment with other luxuries such as an upgraded kitchen with a dishwasher, and added amenities such as private parking and community events. Be fair about whether you are going to use these amenities.

I am entertained by students who choose a housing complex based on amenities, such as a pool, a volleyball court, or a fire pit. Then, after four years of staying in that complex, they realize they did not use any of the amenities. In other words, they wasted hundreds of thousands of dollars.

I've found that students like having the option of using these amenities, but in reality they are unlikely to use them. Again, we are emotional creatures driven by marketing with emotional appeal—not logic. We make emotional purchases and justify them with logic later. Doing the reverse will always benefit you. Thus, justify your purchases and use emotion to feel good about them later.

The closer the housing is to restaurants, stores, and clubs downtown, the higher the cost. Convenience costs are extra. Take the time to assess whether that convenience is worth it. Everything you do should support your goal, provide peace of mind, or contribute to your personal development. Otherwise, the choice is counterproductive.

The number of people you live with will also impact the cost of your living situation. For example, campus housing often has single units that are the most expensive. The more people you get in a room, the lower the cost.

Iowa State University has the Friley dormitory. Friley has single and double living quarters. A single room is almost $1,000 more than a double because one person in their own room takes more space and resources than two people sharing a room.

Let's be honest. If students take full advantage of the college opportunity, they are not spending much time in their dorm room. Studying in the same place where you sleep is not ideal. It is often better to perform the two activities in separate spaces by studying elsewhere, such as in a campus library. Choose a housing situation and ensure it meets your needs; this does not mean you have to go to the cheapest extreme.

Here are a few things to consider before deciding to live off campus:

- First, be very selective about finding a roommate. Not everyone is reliable, and most apartment leases do not have separate agreements for each roommate. If your roommate fails to pay rent, both parties are responsible. In contrast, dormitories typically provide separate contracts for each roommate.
- It may be tempting to room with your best friend and assume they'll never miss a payment. I would not bet on it. Until you live with your best friend and understand their habits and financial mindset, I would steer away from living with friends, to prevent adding stress to the relationship.
- Other things to consider include amenities, a washer and dryer in the unit, the cost of parking, and the cost of utilities, such as garbage, internet, water, electricity, and gas. These are significant costs associated with renting an apartment or a house, and it is critical to understand the responsibilities of the tenant versus those of the owner.

COVID-Disrupted Campus Housing

At the beginning of the COVID-19 pandemic, students got the wake-up call of a lifetime. Many were forced to leave campus housing and relocate in the middle of the spring 2020 semester, but not every student had a positive relationship with family members who could house them. As a result, some universities made exceptions for students who did not have anywhere else to go.

A few universities reimbursed 25 percent of students' housing costs after they had to leave, but most universities did not provide any housing or meal reimbursements. That means the students paid for a benefit they did not receive. After this situation, many colleges added a clause to housing and meal contracts stating that should another unprecedented event occur, the institution would not provide a refund for housing or remaining meals.

Don't Forget Yearly Cost Increases
Regardless of whether you live in campus housing, public housing, or private property, you must gather data about inevitable increases in rent over time. Use a search engine to find housing information. If you're considering university housing, you can look up that data on the university website.

- Gather the cost of accommodation for the past six years. The average cost of housing increases each year.
- The same calculation has to be done for meal plans. Whether buying food from the grocery store or selecting a campus meal plan, it will cost you money. Look up food prices over time to estimate the annual increase.
- Based on the data you gather, estimate the projected costs over the years you will attend to represent the bill better.

The estimated total of high-ticket items is the price of college. This number will help you understand how many scholarships are required to cover the bill and avoid student loan debt.

HOW MUCH FOOD IS ENOUGH?

Campus housing may require you to purchase a meal plan. Verify that the meal plan meets your needs to ensure you get your money's worth. For example, many universities require that traditional dormitory housing be supplemented by a university meal plan; however, most dining centers do not have 24-hour facilities and have limited operating hours. Many students lose money by selecting the wrong meal plan.

Take the following steps to ensure your meal plan meets your needs:

1. Verify when the dining centers are open and compare those times with your schedule. Note when classes occur during one or more open dining-center time blocks.

2. How often do you currently eat? Do not select a meal plan that provides more meals than you typically consume. When selecting a meal plan, try to be realistic about your dietary needs.

3. Before deciding to cook instead of using a meal plan, ask yourself, "Can I cook edible food?" If you can't cook or you find it inconvenient, consider some of the commercial meal plans that ship cooked meals. As a bonus, you might find this kind of light meal prep to be a stress-relieving routine.

4. Eat for nutrition, not comfort.

For the record, eating generic ramen every day is not a suitable diet. An improper diet may decrease your ability to retain new information and perform in the classroom. Before purchasing the cheapest food, think about the health impacts.

College is a six-figure investment, and the price tag can scare people. After you understand the full cost of the opportunity, you should explore how to fund it. The next chapter will dive deeper into the cost of college and how to fund the college commitment.

Siri, play "I Can" by Nas.

Chapter 8

THE PRICE YOU PAY

Education costs money,
but then so does ignorance.
—Claus Moser

A t this point, you know how to select housing, how you will feed yourself, and how long it will take to graduate. Now let's calculate how much it will cost you to get this degree. The average person attending college does not understand the full cost of attendance. They do not understand the impact of the financial investment because they have limited financial literacy and the student loan money is given to the school directly. It is essential to run these numbers and understand the financial investment. It is worth noting that college is the only investment for which a bank will loan six figures to a person who has no source of income or collateral.

IS THE FINANCIAL AID OFFICER RESPONSIBLE FOR HELPING ME GET FUNDING?

A common misconception is that the financial aid officer at a university is responsible for ensuring that the student has sufficient funding. However, these financial aid officers typically do not know information beyond their own university training, which might not be much. Therefore, it is unlikely that they know the intricate details of how the college business works, particularly how to guide families through financial decisions or prevent them from making costly mistakes. Additionally, college financial aid officers are responsible for hundreds, if not thousands, of students. It is unlikely they have enough time to sit down with each student to craft an optimized financial plan suited to the student's needs. Financial aid officers are not in the business of helping students decide if that college is suitable for the long term.

Students must have reasonable expectations regarding their college experience and advocate for themselves if the institution is not delivering on its promise. Often I find students in the consumer mindset, wanting to be accepted, willing to do anything to get into an Ivy League school, only to learn the school is not going to meet their needs, or worse, they cannot afford to finish their degree. These students select the school based on the brand, not necessarily on what it can offer.

WHERE IS THE MONEY?!

Funding college does not have to result in financial ruin, but it requires careful planning. This means finding scholarships and grants. There are multiple levels of scholarship applications.

- Local level: Banks, high schools, and nonprofits usually have scholarships available. Many people avoid local scholarships because their payout is not high, often ranging from $500 to $1,500. While it does not seem like a lot of money, these amounts add up very quickly. If this were a job and it took two hours to complete a $500 scholarship application, the applicant would make $250 per hour. Unless you make $250 per hour at a job, you should apply for these $500 scholarships as well. These scholarships are often easier to obtain than big-money scholarships because the applicant pool is usually small.

- County level: Some organizations and nonprofits give scholarships to people who live in a particular county and meet specific criteria. County scholarships are often easier to get than the state scholarships.

- State level: Qualifying for these scholarships requires the applicant to be a resident of a particular state. The scholarships are not automatically awarded and still require applications.

- University level: These may be available through a department, college, or alumni association. Alumni donate money throughout the year to these funds. Some scholarships may not require students to prove financial need. Email the alumni association monthly to inquire about new scholarships.

- National level: These are extremely difficult to win, and your application must be pristine. I don't mean to discourage you from pursuing these scholarships, but I do want to be transparent. These scholarships typically cover all tuition. Examples are the Bill and Melinda Gates Scholarship, the Coca-Cola Scholarship, and the Gates Millennium Scholars Program.

The smaller the organization sponsoring the scholarship, the easier the money is to obtain. It's a numbers game; play the odds and do not take any rejection personally.

Most people do not spend adequate time searching and applying for scholarships. Still, now that you understand what you're getting yourself into, you may have more incentive to apply for every opportunity available.

Most scholarships require an essay. As somebody who's now on the other side evaluating applications and helping select awardees, I've noticed that many essays do not answer the essay prompt. Fantastic stories that do not explicitly state the connection between the story and the application prompt are not awarded money. If a scholarship application deadline is extended, assume there are not enough applicants—in plain English, there are more scholarships than people who applied. That's free money waiting for you!

If there is competition, leverage personal life experiences to win scholarships. These experiences can look like milestones or turning points in your life where you learned you have specific identities; unfortunate events and disadvantages in life are scholarship-essay material. The crucial part of this formula is to reframe those events in a positive light. It is essential to tell the story in such a way that demonstrates your growth. Each disadvantage must come with an equal advantage.

This is the scholarship process for the "hero" story:

- A winning scholarship essay clearly states the lesson learned within the first two or three sentences. Starting with the lesson learned and explicitly stating the connection to the scholarship question decreases the chance that the scholarship reviewer will misinterpret the essay.
- Following that, tell a story about how a situation caused a setback. Include vivid details for emotional appeal. While

it is acceptable to be vulnerable, avoid disclosing anything that makes you feel uncomfortable. The process may feel like self-reflection. The key is to be authentic. Avoid exaggerating the story and making up facts.

- The essay should always end positively, stating the lessons learned and the impact of the events.
- Avoid stories about athletics where you did not achieve a particular position, a breakup, and not being valedictorian, as these are common stories used by high school students and do not have a return on investment.

Scholarships are not the only way to pay for college. Grants are federal or state-funded awards given to students of selected criteria. However, the distribution of the awards may be at the university's discretion. Often this money is given out on a first-come, first-served basis. Therefore, complete the financial aid application as early as possible to capitalize on the opportunity.

I Don't Qualify for Financial Aid! Now What?
Some companies will pay for you to get an education if you agree to work for them for some years after obtaining your degree. These programs are called tuition assistance programs. After you earn your degree, a company may require a work commitment equivalent to the years you accepted tuition assistance. This can often be a win-win because the company may offer training and you can avoid incurring student loan debt. I have seen plenty of students take part in these programs as part-time or full-time employees or as a co-op. A co-op (cooperative education) combines classroom education with work directly related to the field of study.

In contrast, an internship is a work experience that typically lasts 10 to 12 weeks. As shown in the table below, there are important differences between an internship and a co-op. The time commitment and the pay are the key differences to note.

What's the Difference?		
Experience Type	Co-op	Internship
Duration	3+ months	6+ weeks
Pay	Yes	Not always
Training	Focused; skills acquired directly relate to the field	Explorative; may not be an accurate representation of full-time work
University Restrictions	Not typically	Yes

Lisa Marisa did not qualify for financial aid. Her parents refused to support her education financially. She did a series of co-ops for Rockwell Collins as an electrical engineering intern while taking advantage of the employee tuition-reimbursement program to pay for courses while she worked. Lisa was a full-time student for one semester and paid out of pocket using the funds saved from her co-op. Then, she did another co-op for nine months while simultaneously taking courses funded by her employer. Lisa oscillated between employer-paid and self-paid classes until graduation. Although it took Lisa seven years to complete her degree, she did it without debt and gained years of engineering experience.

The other option I have seen students choose is an employer-paid education while working full-time. After high school, Ashley landed a job as an administrator at a national laboratory. She was unclear about her career path but needed to support herself until she figured it out. She decided she wanted to become a cyber analyst. Ashley leveraged the supplemental tuition reimbursement program from her employer to pay for all her education while working as an admin. She worked during the day and took classes in the evening. After two years of courses, Ashley's employer began transitioning her into cyber-related projects. She completed her bachelor's in cybersecurity in three more years and transitioned to being a full-time cyber analyst without debt.

The ideal situation is gaining experience while simultaneously taking courses to build up the skill set necessary for full-time employment. In addition, internship experience provides a more comprehensive understanding of the job requirements than just reading the job description. Through experience, I have found that jobs typically require more than is listed in the description.

Anyone questioning their field should pursue an internship as soon as possible. The experience will provide a more accurate representation than courses alone. In addition, internship experiences should be used to explore potential career fields, while co-ops should be used to get more training in a chosen field.

Accepting the Risk of Student Loans

Some people make the mistake of feeling comfortable with student loan debt. They assume they will be able to repay their debt within ten years of graduating. Unfortunately, these are often individuals who have not sat down and taken the time to calculate the monthly payments and their own cost of living. These students do not know when the interest will begin to accumulate on the loans.

Student loans are extremely dangerous, primarily because of how interest is calculated.

A good majority of Americans have student loan debt, so chances are you know someone who does too. During the pandemic, collective student loan debt hit a new high of $1.7 trillion. It is the second-highest debt in the United States, after mortgage debt.

Government student loans carry lower interest rates than private loans do. Private-lender interest rates are drastically higher, sometimes two to three times the federal student loan rate.

Don't Chase Recognition

You must value your education. Too often we pursue things based on the reaction of others. It is nice when other people, such as your family or significant others, celebrate your accomplishments, but you should also have a genuine interest in the things you pursue. If you do not plan for life, it will happen to you.

Ashutosh and his family gave up everything to come to the United States. His family constantly reminded Ashutosh of their sacrifices. When he was seven, his parents started telling him he had to become a doctor—after all, that was the only thing they thought would bring the family pride. So he felt the pressure to be a doctor, even though that wasn't really what he wanted to do. He did it anyway. Ashutosh suffered through his undergrad and graduate studies, finishing at the head of his class, but he remained unhappy. Despite having no interest in being a medical doctor, he completed the residency program. He also married the woman his family selected for him. Ashutosh obtained a job at a hospital, and the hospital agreed to repay his student loans after ten years of employment.

He was living the life his parents had chosen for him, but of course he wasn't happy. A few years passed, and his career started to weigh on him. Ashutosh began casually drinking after work to cope with the stress. Eventually, he started drinking on the job. Before he knew it, Ashutosh was performing surgery while intoxicated, and he made a mistake that killed a patient. Within a week, he lost his job, he was barred from ever practicing medicine again, and his wife left him. Everything he had worked so hard for was gone. Even his family disowned him.

After losing so much, Ashutosh hit rock bottom.

To make matters worse, he still had student loan debt—and no way to repay it. To find himself, he started meditating; as a result, he grew interested in carpentry. It turned out he was very good at this work and very passionate about it. Ashutosh secured an apprenticeship, where he learned to perfect his craft. Despite his dire situation, he'd found something to bring himself peace of mind. Fast-forward five years, and Ashutosh had become one of the best carpenters in his field, making more money than he'd ever made as a doctor. One year later, he repaid his student loan debt and repaired his relationship with his parents.

Sometimes we choose a career because our parents want it, not because we want it. Unfortunately, the pressure associated with family pride can lead to disastrous outcomes. Before pursuing a degree or occupation to make your parents happy, make sure that it's what you want—because if you don't like it, you will not be able to hold on to success, if you even get any at all.

STUDENT LOANS (SO, WHAT'S THE BIG DEAL?)

Student loan debt can get out of hand very quickly. Federal student loans are preferred over private ones because the government typically offers a much lower interest rate. The interest rate and compounding frequency matter! Failure to understand compound interest can cause financial ruin. Let's look into the connection between compound interest and student loans.

Federal student loans come in three types: subsidized, unsubsidized, and Parent PLUS loans. *Subsidized* implies that the loan will not incur interest while you are at least a half-time student. *Unsubsidized* means that while the student is in school, the loan will incur interest starting the day the loan is disbursed to the student. A Parent PLUS loan is a loan taken out by the parent to be used for their child's education, meaning it will be the parent's responsibility to pay the loan back, and the loan will show up on their credit report. In contrast, subsidized and unsubsidized loans will be the student's responsibility and will show up on their credit report. However, federally backed loans limit how much a student can borrow, as shown in the table below. These limits are based on the expected family contribution (EFC), calculated using data the student enters in the Free Application for Federal Student Aid (FAFSA) form. The EFC determines how much money the student and their family are expected to contribute to financing the student's education.

Direct Unsubsidized Loan Limits 2022–2023				
Year	Annual Limit	Amount Borrowed	Aggregate Debt	Remaining Aggregate Loan Eligibility
First Year (Freshman)	$5,500	$5,500	$5,500	$25,500
Second Year (Sophomore)	$6,500	$6,500	$12,000	$19,000
Third Year (Junior)	$7,500	$7,500	$19,500	$11,500
Fourth Year (Senior)	$7,500	$7,500	$27,000	$4,000
Fifth Year (Senior)	$7,500	$4,000	$31,000	$0

The direct unsubsidized loan has annual limits for dependent undergraduate students based on the student's year in school.

Financial aid award letters list the types of financing available to the student and the Cost of Attendance (COA). For example, the financial aid sources could include student loans, grants, work-study programs, EFC, and the amount of financial aid the college contributes. In addition, colleges offer students discounts through scholarships, which colleges are more likely to provide to families that they believe will donate money to the school. As a result, the university's endowment fund may indicate the college's flexibility in negotiating costs.

Yes, you read that correctly. The financial award letter can be negotiated, which is called *appealing the award of financial assistance*. Higher education is well known for using language that high schoolers do not understand, which may make many students feel overwhelmed.

Finding a student who understands the financial investment of college is difficult, partially because many students come directly from high school and do not understand the value of money, nor do they know the impact of compound interest. Most high school students do not work a job to cover living expenses or have credit cards. Therefore, I feel it is unrealistic to expect them to understand compound interest or the value of money.

Obtaining student loans is a choice made by the borrower. Therefore, it is the borrower's responsibility to repay a loan as agreed. Student loans are the only form of six-figure debt that can be obtained without merit, credit score, or relevant qualifications, and with zero underwriting. Things get dangerous because most students do not understand their financial commitment. For most people, college will be their second-largest investment next to purchasing a home. If you would not buy a home without a real estate agent to guide you, I strongly discourage you from going to college without someone to guide you through the process. Student loans can result in financial ruin, but a lack of understanding of compound interest causes the most pain. The Rule of 72 is an excellent shortcut to understanding the impact of compound interest.

UNDERSTANDING COMPOUND INTEREST — THE RULE OF 72

The Rule of 72 estimates how long it will take for compound interest to double the investment or debt. To use the rule, divide 72 by the interest rate to get the average amount of time it will take for a loan to double. This rule becomes very important when calculating student loan debt and understanding why so many students struggle to repay their debt. First, let's look into how student loan debt can cause financial ruin. For the record, student loan debt is the only debt that is virtually impossible to remove via bankruptcy.

Carter is a high school English teacher with a salary of $35,000, and he owes $20,000 in student loans. He lives with his two kids and partner. For a federal subsidized loan, the standard monthly amount required to repay the loan within ten years is $83.17. However, Carter has two children and cannot afford the loan payment. So let's look at the Rule of 72 for each loan to see how this might impact him.

Loan Program	Federal Subsidized Loan
Annual Interest Rate	4.99%
Original Loan Amount (Principal Amount)	$20,000
Rule of 72	14.43 years

72 / Annual Interest Rate = Years for a loan to double
72 / 4.99% = 14.43 years

Based on the table, the federal subsidized loan would take 14.43 years to double if no payments were made. However, it's better to pay something rather than nothing. The federal subsidized loan is government backed, and the government offers an income-based repayment program. Based on his income and number of dependents (two), Carter qualifies for a monthly payment of $61, which is at least $61 per month cheaper than his scheduled standard repayment plan, as shown in the table below.

Let's see the impact of compound interest by viewing his debt under different student loan programs. To meet his repayment obligations in the agreed-upon time frame of ten years for the subsidized loan, Carter would need to pay $212.03 per month, where $128.87 goes toward paying down the principal amount, and $83.17 goes toward paying the interest. However, the income-based repayment plan has reduced his payments to $61 per month. The new income-driven payment of $61 is not enough to cover the interest payment of $83.17. This means that all of Carter's payments are going toward interest and will not decrease his loan amount because interest is paid first and anything left over is paid toward the principal amount. Here is where compound interest becomes a problem. At a minimum, Carter would need to pay the entire interest amount to prevent the total loan amount from increasing. However, his new payment plan will not meet his minimum interest amount. As a result, the total loan amount will never decrease. This means the income repayment plan will cause Carter to owe more money than originally borrowed. But how?

I'm glad you asked! Every year the unpaid interest that has accumulated will be added to the principal amount; this is the compounding part. Carter's payment does not cover the monthly interest accumulated. Therefore, none of the payments go toward the original loan amount of $20,000. After a year, any unpaid interest is added to the principal, and a new principal amount is created. The new principal amount is used to calculate the next month's interest and dramatically speeds up the loan's cost. This is how many people get trapped and cannot get out.

Remember the Rule of 72? For the subsidized loan, the Rule of 72 stated that the loan would double every 14.43 years if no payments were made. As shown in the table below, various student loan programs have different interest rates. As a result, the minimum monthly repayment amount will vary.

Student Loan Programs				
	Federal Subsidized Loan	Federal Unsubsidized Loan	Parent PLUS Loan	Private Loan
Annual Interest Rate	4.99	6.54	7.54	11.8
Original Loan Amount	$20,000	$20,000	$20,000	$20,000
Years to Double Debt (Rule of 72)	14.43	11	9.55	6.1
Monthly Minimum to Repay Loan in 10 Years	$212.03	$227.50	$237.82	$284.63
Adjusted Income Payment	$61	$61	$61	$61

Note that a private loan would take 6.1 years to double without payments, meaning that the debt will increase twice as fast as a subsidized loan. This should make you feel uncomfortable. Essentially, you have less time to repay the debt. The higher the interest, the quicker the amount will double. Now you understand why private student loans are discouraged; the interest rates are usually double that of federal rates. Compound interest also impacts credit cards, mortgages, and car loans, among other financial instruments. Credit-card interest rates range from 10 percent to 25 percent. Using the Rule of 72, credit-card debt would double every 7.2 years at 10 percent, and every 2.88 years at 25 percent. Credit-card debt is financial suicide!

I digress; let's get to student loans. Student loans can be avoided in college if you are intelligent about navigating financial decisions. This means strategically moving through college and selecting courses for the ideal position at your target company. When you're clear about what you're doing and why you're doing it, you know why you must remain diligent and persistent. Without this clarity, you're randomly stumbling through an academic program that doesn't seem to have much value to you.

While it may be tempting to depend on the government to rescue you from student loan debt, I would not rely on it. Politicians have made many promises only to break them. Should there be some relief from the government, it may not be much. Therefore, I strongly discourage anyone from assuming their student loan debt will be repaid by someone else.

Siri, play "Options" by NF.

Outro

Some Final Thoughts About College

When you get in debt you become a slave.
—Andrew Jackson

COLLEGE ISN'T FOR EVERYONE

At some point, society pressures high school students to go directly to college, without giving them adequate informa-tion. I do not believe everyone needs to go to college. However, there are benefits available for everyone who does, if new students know how to use them. Personally, I believe there is nothing wrong with *not* going to college. Just know that you will pay for information whether you attend college or not. Some people pay a university for information; some purchase a boot-camp course; some purchase books; some pay for masterminds; and others pay with their time. Knowledge must be obtained, but the source is irrelevant.

There is only one limitation that humans have: the self-imposed limitation we create within our minds.

Understand that every opportunity has risks. Some risks may not be as extreme as others, but they do exist. Some people seek absolute job security, but frankly, that idea is unrealistic. A degree will not guarantee you a job. But with some perspective and a clear purpose, you can be a successful student and launch a thriving career.

WHAT IS THE VALUE OF COLLEGE, ANYWAY?

If you decide to pursue a degree, you must choose a college that fits your needs. Remember, each college has unique attributes that no other kind of organization has at such a large scale. Namely, these four main benefits are underused: 1) intellectual capital (knowledge), 2) social capital (network), 3) financial capital (scholarships), and 4) assets (resources). Paying someone to teach you how to use these benefits to your advantage is worth the investment. University networks span generations. The college most likely has alumni or staff members who could be a mentor in any endeavor you select.

Furthermore, everyone can leverage college to accelerate their career. However, this leverage requires careful planning before attending college. Students may decide to terminate their degree if they begin to generate a source of income sufficient to support themselves before graduation. The degree is insurance for your career but not a requirement.

WHAT DO COLLEGES LOOK FOR
IN AN IDEAL STUDENT?

College is a business, but most people do not see that until after they have acquired student loan debt. Despite popular belief, most schools do not value grades that much. Being a "good" student is insufficient evidence that you will have a thriving career. A school's reputation is based on the career success of their alumni. The goal is not the degree! The goal is to leverage college as a platform to accelerate your career.

Institutions need students who demonstrate the potential to have promising careers. At the end of the day, a college is only as good as its alumni. Therefore, colleges need their students to have impressive careers for the institution to continue to have clout. This means prospective students must succinctly communicate how they plan to leverage the college to catapult their careers. These institutions want to increase their number of distinguished alumni. An attractive prospective student can identify a problem they wish to solve, explain its impact on society, and explain why the institution selected is the perfect fit.

Financial predators prey on those who are ignorant. Take time to educate yourself about the college you plan to attend, the resources available, alumni connections, and faculty/staff expertise. It may seem like an overwhelming amount of work, and you may want someone else to deal with it. However, when you allow someone else to take over your financial responsibilities, they may not be as diligent as you would be. Simply put, it's not their money! Therefore, assuming that someone else will make decisions on your behalf and carefully examine the financial implications of each decision is unrealistic.

Most college marketing is geared toward making students feel as if they are included and wanted. This message will often cause students to attend colleges that do not fit their needs, which drastically increases the chances of students dropping out.

WILL GOING TO AN IVY LEAGUE SCHOOL GUARANTEE JOB SECURITY?

Nope. To be frank, many rankings are based on graduate-school publications and citations, not undergraduate performance. Therefore, if you have no plans to obtain a master's or doctorate, the rankings should not mean much to you. Furthermore, many high-ranking institutions are focused on research, not on helping their undergrads get jobs.

These top schools are brands, and Ivy League schools are brands typically named after people. Harvard University is named after John Harvard; Yale University is named after Elihu Yale; Cornell University is named after Ezra Cornell; and Brown University is named after Nicholas Brown. Do not be so quick or proud to prioritize these names over your own family name. I believe that by yearning to be accepted into these institutions, you are saying that you want to be affiliated with someone else's family more than your own. Chances are, you have a last name. To be blunt, your last name is a brand; act accordingly. Nicholas Brown: "To be affiliated with a brand that is already well known is a partnership, and should you play your cards right, it will work in your favor. However, do not be so quick or proud."

Don't be foolish and think that success will happen overnight, or even that you will be wildly successful after two years of college. While a short turnaround may have worked for Bill Gates, it is unlikely to work for everyone. This is not to discourage anyone but instead to be realistic.

STUDENT LOANS (LET'S BE REAL: YOU DON'T HAVE THAT MONEY!)

A common misconception for many students is that once they obtain a college degree, they will have a job waiting for them without putting in additional effort.

However, many students are left feeling frustrated, betrayed, and lied to when they graduate with student loan debt and no job. They feel they were promised a job if they got the degree and did the work, but the process is a bit more complicated than that. Unfortunately, the key benefits of college weren't explicitly discussed in the most transparent manner.

For many people, college is the most expensive investment they will ever make in themselves and the largest project they will ever complete. Naturally, it can seem overwhelming. The key is to take it one step at a time, and before you know it, you'll be done. Play the odds in your favor and make decisions based on facts to diminish risks and fear. Get past your fear of pursuing your goal.

Pushing past my fears has allowed me to build platforms dedicated to teaching people how to properly navigate the decisions of college and become an indispensable employee. It has given me the freedom to pursue my risky passions. I wrote this book to help you do the same. You now have a solid understanding of how to navigate college decisions and choose to your advantage. You also know that college mistakes can cost you thousands of dollars per mistake. With this knowledge, you can avoid panic and focus on your goal. You are responsible for your success. If you fail to plan and make strategic decisions, you may drastically decrease the value of your investment.

SUCCESS WON'T HAPPEN OVERNIGHT

Your success will not be immediate. Instantaneous success rarely happens. In fact, real, sustainable change takes time. There may be moments when you feel stuck, but growth is nonlinear—you may have some ups and downs. Trust the process and appreciate the journey. Be gentle with yourself and be kind, even when you feel impatient. Define success for yourself. Living life on someone else's terms will most likely end in self-sabotage and destruction. Your college experience must be completed on your terms and measured by your definition of success.

HOW TO START YOUR COLLEGE JOURNEY

Ready, set, go! Here are a few tips to help you get started.

- Time management: We are inundated with technology and software constantly battling for our attention. As a millennial who grew up with Facebook and instant messaging, I completely understand how easy it is to get distracted and wonder where the day went. For this reason, I recommend working on college materials in select spaces where you do not bring your cell phone or log in to social media. Additionally, I recommend scheduling 30 minutes daily to complete activities.
- Ritual: To increase the chances of staying on track, make working on college material a part of your daily schedule. You may have an action that triggers your mind to start work, such as making tea in the morning.
- Organization: Make sure that you have everything organized. Applying for college is ultimately one of the most significant projects you will ever complete. The process

is more personally invasive than purchasing a home or getting married. Schools assume students are dependent on their parents and require details about their finances. Many things must be tracked, and each college may require something different.

- Checklists: There are complimentary checklists to help you navigate the college process. These checklists will help ensure that you are asking the right questions to identify unnecessary costs. For access to these checklists go to ManufacturedEducation.com/checklist.

- Coaching: Do not do this alone. Applying for college is overwhelming; one mistake could cost you thousands. A coach is there to keep you on track and help you navigate the complexities of higher education. Additionally, a coach will hold you accountable and track your progress.

I am so proud of you for having the courage to be accountable for your success. You recognize the impact that college could have on your future, and you are doing everything in your power to maximize your opportunities.

Now, let's keep moving forward. And remember, this is a marathon, not a sprint.

Siri, play "All I Do Is Win" by DJ Khaled.

If you gained anything valuable from this book, please head over to Amazon and leave a review.

For permission requests and bulk-order purchase options, email info@ManufacturedEducation.com.

For speaking inquiries, email info@CimoneSpeaks.com.

WORK WITH CIMONE AND HER TEAM

We have a coaching program that helps students navigate the decisions of college and obtain a full-time job offer before graduation.

If you want to know more about this program and see if you qualify, apply at the website shown below and schedule a call.

Coaching Program: https://workwith.heycimone.com/

Connect with Cimone

 Hey_Cimone

 HeyCimone

 Hey_Cimone

About the Author

In 2010, a life-altering event led Dr. W to discover the benefits of higher education and leverage them to accelerate her personal growth, career, and brand recognition. While discovering this, she developed the concept of Manufactured Education, a set of essential resources and principles to help students mindfully navigate their college opportunities. When not busy studying cybersecurity, Dr. W studies the velocity of money.

Dr. W is a two-time recovering underachiever, serial entrepreneur, technophile, and professional troublemaker. Using her business expertise and student and teaching experience, she demystifies the collegiate processes by closing the information gap. She provides actionable steps to help students maximize their college experiences, find internships, and transform into indispensable employees. As a highly sought-after coach, consultant, and speaker, she frequently shares her proven strategies and tactics with people all over the world.

Dr. W can be contacted directly via email at Cimone@ HeyCimone.com.

Made in the USA
Columbia, SC
19 February 2024

31807796R00078